BIBLE
PERSONALITIES

BIBLE
PERSONALITIES

A Treasury of Insights for
Personal Growth and Ministry

WARREN W. WIERSBE

BakerBooks

Grand Rapids, Michigan

© 2005 by Warren W. Wiersbe

Published by Baker Books
a division of Baker Publishing Group
P.O. Box 6287, Grand Rapids, MI 49516-6287
www.bakerbooks.com

Printed in the United States of America

Library of Congress Cataloging-in-Publication Data
Wiersbe, Warren W.
        Bible personalities : a treasury of insights for personal growth and ministry / Warren W.
    Wiersbe.
            p.   cm.
        Includes bibliographical references.
        ISBN 0-8010-6526-7 (pbk.)
        1. Bible—Biography—Dictionaries. I. Title.
    BS570.W57 2005
    220.9′2—dc22   2004021440

CONTENTS

PART I

THE
BIOGRAPHICAL
SERMON

I

BIOGRAPHICAL PREACHING IS IMPORTANT

A biographical sermon is a sermon that explains and applies biblical truth to life today on the basis of texts that cluster around a Bible personality.

While this definition doesn't eliminate the people in our Lord's parables or those described in the book of Proverbs, our emphasis in this book will be on flesh-and-blood characters with real histories, even if the inspired writers left them anonymous. The gifted Scottish preacher Alexander Whyte preached messages about the characters in our Lord's parables, the "angels" of the seven churches in Asia Minor, and even the personalities in John Bunyan's *Pilgrim's Progress*. But Whyte had a uniquely sanctified imagination that most of us admire but probably cannot imitate.

Let's emphasize real messages about real people—what they were like, what they experienced, how they changed (for better or for worse), how they handled the circumstances of life, how they related to other people, and, most of all, how they related to God. We want to know what they contributed to the salvation story that is the overriding theme of Scripture. Most of all, we want to know what they can teach us today.

One of the most successful preachers of Bible biography was Clarence Edward Macartney, whose many sermon books you should add to your library. He wrote in the foreword to *The Wisest Fool, and Other Men of the Bible,* "I discovered early in my ministry that people like biography; and nowhere is there such biography, so stirring, so moving, so uplifting, so tragic, as that to be found in the Bible."[1] He wrote those words in 1949. By that time, he had preached 167 biographical sermons—and there were many more to follow! In Macartney's delightful autobiography *The Making of a Minister,* he tells how he "discovered" Bible biography while serving as a summer intern during his student days. "I had only a few books with me . . . and had it not been for the Old Testament characters, I would have gone into pulpit bankruptcy. . . . That experience taught me the appeal of biographical preaching, and thus opened for me a rich pulpit vein that I am still working."[2]

The Bible is basically a dramatic history book, and, as A. T. Pierson said, "History is His story." Scripture records the great salvation narrative, which employs a cast of thousands of characters who reveal human nature at its best and its worst. It shows how God worked in and through these individuals to reveal his mercy and love. The main message of the Bible is the grace of God as seen in Jesus Christ, the good news that Jesus can change people and make them new creatures.[3]

We preach Bible biography because we preach the Bible and cannot avoid the characters who inhabit its pages. People today are intensely interested in other people, especially those they admire and perhaps envy. Consider the success of the Biography Channel, *Biography* magazine, *People* magazine, and celebrity interviews. Add to these the popularity of biographies and autobiographies sold in bookstores. "The only value of a life is its content—*for others,*" wrote Dag Hammarskjöld in his spiritual autobiography *Mark- ings.*[4] Each life has content, and the lives of Bible personalities are especially rich. Listen to an interview with the average showbiz celebrity and you quickly discover there isn't much content; then listen to an interview with a real leader, scholar, saint, or hero, and you move into the depths of character and relationships.

The life content of the people found in the Bible will constantly challenge you, not only as a Christian but also as a servant of the

Lord. After completing his monumental biography of Robert E. Lee, Douglas Freeman said, "I have been fully repaid by being privileged to live . . . for more than a decade in the company of a great gentleman." What moral and spiritual strength we preachers ought to receive as we walk with Abraham, Moses, David, and Paul!

If it is done correctly, biographical preaching is especially effective because it combines story, practical psychology, and biblical theology, all wrapped up in the lives of real people. Biographical sermons rescue congregations from having to wrestle with abstract ideas and dull historical facts from the pulpit that seem to have no connection with real life. When you preach Bible biography, you show what God can do with ordinary people in real-life situations, and this tells your congregation what God can do for them today. Our message is not about what God did for David centuries ago but what God is doing for his people today. Eugene Peterson reminds us that "we are living in the middle of a story that was begun and will be concluded by another. And that other is God."[5]

In an interview with Bill Moyers, Canadian literary critic Northrup Frye said: "The Bible to me is not a structure of doctrine, not a structure of propositions, but a collection of stories making up one single story, and that's the interrelationship of God and man."[6] In preaching biographical messages, wise preachers can expound Bible doctrine and teach propositional truth without the listener realizing they are doing it. In one dramatic biblical episode after another, we can confront our listeners with what Scripture describes as "the world," that diabolical system that is opposed to God and blinds people to the truth. From Lot and Abraham in Genesis to the fall of godless Babylon in Revelation, the Bible exposes the falseness and futility of the illusion that is the world system. The unbeliever says that something is as sure as the world, but John says that the world is passing away (1 John 2:17)! By teaching about Bible personalities, we can expose sin, magnify God's grace, and deal with neglected themes that today's congregations need to hear.

Bible culture is vastly different from modern culture, but the Bible world is the same world that tempts Christians today. Good biographical preaching will reach people right where they are as they wrestle with the world, the flesh, and the devil. Decades ago seminary professors called this "life-situation preaching," but biographical preaching does more than tell people how to face and solve problem situations in life. It goes much deeper and deals with motives, illusions, and evasions, the lies that impel people to make the unwise decisions that cause their lives to fall apart. Dysfunctional families existed in the pages of the Bible long before the term itself became popular in the literature of modern psychology.

One word of caution: please don't announce that biographical preaching makes the Bible "come alive." The Bible is alive whether we preach it or not (Heb. 4:12; 1 Peter 1:23), and poorly prepared biographical sermons can be as dead as any other kind of bad preaching. Good biographical sermons can convince our listeners that the living Word of God meets them where they are and, if believed and obeyed, helps to get them where God wants them to be. Remember, effective biographical sermons are about present reality, not ancient history. They focus on what God wants to do for his people today and not what he did for Israel centuries ago.

2

BIOGRAPHICAL PREACHING IS SERIOUS

Since we represent a holy God and preach from a holy book, and since the consequences involve life and death, all preaching is serious. But preaching Bible biography is especially so and, to quote the traditional marriage ceremony, "must not be entered into lightly or carelessly, but soberly and in the fear of God." The analogy is an instructive one, for in preparing a biographical sermon, we "marry" our minds and hearts to what we know about the minds and hearts of Bible personalities, and we "live with them" as we learn from them. The people we preach about may be strangers to the congregation, but they had better not be strangers to us. If our preparation is careless and hurried, we may end up committing one of two sins: bearing false witness against one of the Lord's servants by teaching error, or teaching truth in a manner that makes us act superior to the person about whom we're preaching.

I once heard a high-profile preacher say to a large congregation, "You'll recognize Peter when you get to heaven. He's the fellow with the foot-shaped mouth." The people around me laughed, but my heart was heavy. There isn't a preacher alive who is worthy to carry Peter's sandals let alone ridicule him in public. Let's try to practice the Golden Rule as we preach. Let's speak about Bible personalities the way we would want them to speak about us, which means, let's be loving and let's be fair. The people we preach about are real people, created in the image of God. We're dealing with flesh and blood, not paper and ink.

Biographical preaching is serious because we're dealing with that elusive thing called *character*. We don't fully understand our own hearts let alone the hearts of people who walked this earth millenniums ago. We boastfully say, "Well, if I know my own heart"—but we *don't* know our own hearts! After all, Jeremiah 17:9 is still in the Bible: "The heart is deceitful above all things and beyond cure. Who can understand it?" Phillips Brooks said that the purpose of life is the shaping of character by truth, a process that is not easy. "The conversion of a soul is the miracle of a moment," wrote Alan Redpath, "the manufacture of a saint is the task of a lifetime."[1] The understanding of a human being may also be the task of a lifetime. "We are always sowing our future; we are always reaping our past," wrote W. R. Inge, the "gloomy dean" of St. Paul's Cathedral, and only God knows the condition of the soil and the promise of the harvest.[2]

When it comes to human nature, the world's thinkers and leaders are either very optimistic or very pessimistic. The year I was born, people were singing, "So always look for the silver lining / And try to find the sunny side of life"; but that same year the Crash occurred and brought the near economic ruin of the nation. The esteemed historian Barbara Tuchman told Bill Moyers in a television interview, "Revolutions produce other men, not new men. Halfway between truth and endless error, the mold of the species is permanent. That is earth's burden."[3] But Christians are realists. While they have little or no faith in human nature alone, they do believe that God can implant new life in people's hearts and empower them to help change the lives of others. The Bible tells stories of men and women who were utterly transformed by the grace of God, and these stories need to be told again and again. Abram became Abraham, Sarai became Sarah, Jacob became Israel, Saul of Tarsus became Paul the apostle, and Simon became Peter. Christian realists are pessimistic about human nature but optimistic about the power and grace of the Lord.

God's goal for his people is that they become more and more like Jesus Christ, what Paul called "conformed to the likeness of his Son" (Rom. 8:29). "For we are God's workmanship" (Eph. 2:10), which suggests that God has to work *in* us before he can work *through* us. Spirit-empowered preaching is one of his most important tools. Preach about how God worked in frightened Gideon and made him a mighty man of valor and you will encourage many believers who are closet cowards. It's serious work to build character and seek to make people more like Jesus, but it's also joyful work that lasts for eternity. In short, biographical preaching is worth the effort expended in the study, the prayer closet, and the pulpit.

3

Biographical Preaching Requires a Prepared Preacher

Phillips Brooks's familiar definition of preaching in his *Lectures on Preaching* as "the bringing of truth through personality" is especially applicable to biographical preaching. We can't bring a sincere message if our inner person hasn't connected in a deeper way with the inner person of the Bible character we are focusing on. It's easier to grasp a subtle argument in one of Paul's epistles than to identify with the Israelites at the Red Sea or with the apostles when the risen Christ suddenly appeared in a locked room. Beware the false confidence that arises in your heart when you say, "I know just how they felt!" Perhaps you do, or perhaps your imagination is a bit overheated. One reason why the Lord permits his servants to suffer is to help us better understand what other people really go through, and then be prepared to encourage them (2 Cor. 1:1–11). Listen again to Phillips Brooks: "To be a true minister to men is always to accept new happiness and new distress, both of them forever deepening and entering into closer and more inseparable union with each other the more profound and spiritual the ministry becomes. The man who gives himself to other men can never be a wholly sad man; but no more can he be a man of unclouded gladness."[1] Ministry is a land of hills and valleys.

We study the men and women of the Bible, not the way an impatient husband observes people in a shopping mall as he waits for his wife but the way an oncologist examines cells under a microscope as he searches for cancer. The husband is an amused but uninvolved spectator; the doctor is an involved caregiver who is dealing with life and death. As we prepare to wield the sword of the Spirit, we must realize that the Word both hurts and heals, and we must strive to keep our ministry balanced.

The Biblical personalities we preach about have all been dead for centuries, yet they are part of God's living Word, and we must be careful how we examine their lives and "operate" on their hearts. Let's seek to treat these Bible characters the way the Lord treats us. The sins we see in others may be reflections of our own weaknesses and we must deal with them honestly. Biographical preaching requires the skill of the surgeon and the compassion of a mother, as well as the honesty of the scientist. If we want to speak the truth in love (Eph. 4:15), we must also study the truth in love. Our purpose is not to be sensational. The sword of the Spirit cuts only that the poison may be removed and the wound healed by God's grace.

We must be honest with the Lord and with ourselves if we want to minister compassionately to our people; but honesty, humility, and compassion are essentials for every sermon that we preach. Perhaps this was one of Alexander Whyte's secrets in biographical preaching: he first examined his own heart and dealt with his own sins, learned from the Bible character he was studying, and then turned the laser beam of truth on the congregation. In John Kelman's tribute to Whyte, he said, "He preached nothing beyond the terrors and the glories among which his own heart had trembled or rejoiced. . . . He spoke no generalities, and was always thinking of living men and women. Apparently the simplest of men, he was yet also the shrewdest in his judgments, and you took your life in hand when you went to hear him preach."[2]

In his sermon on "Paul, the Chief of Sinners," Whyte told his congregation, "My true classics now are those masterly men who look into their own hearts and then write for my heart."[3] The lower we are before God, the clearer we see both ourselves and the people in the Bible. "A real book is not one that's read, but one that reads us," wrote poet W. H. Auden, and the Bible certainly qualifies. Another gifted biographical preacher, F. W. Robertson, agrees with Whyte and Auden: "You cannot unveil the secrets of another heart without at the same time finding something to correspond with, and perchance explain, the mysteries of your own. Heart answers here to heart."[4] Without honesty and humility, we step into the pulpit as judges and prosecuting attorneys, and not as Good Samaritans ready to share both the antiseptic wine and the soothing oil.

Like Simon the Pharisee (Luke 7:36–50), some of us are prone to classify people by their past deeds instead of by their deeper desires and their future potential. Taught to exercise discernment, most preachers want to classify people rather than leave all judgments to the Lord from whom nothing can be hidden. King Ahab was a sinner of sinners who "sold [himself] to do evil" (1 Kings 21:20, 25 NKJV), and yet the Lord postponed sending judgment because Ahab repented. Barnabas is called "a good man" (Acts 11:24) and yet he joined Peter in lapsing into legalism (Gal. 2:11–13). To be sure, it's better to focus on the steady course of a person's life than to camp on one unfortunate failure, but we have to face the fact that many Bible heroes failed even in their strengths. Abraham's faith failed and he fled to Egypt, and there he failed again when he started to lie. Moses lost his meekness and then lost his temper. David abandoned his integrity and tried to cover up his sins. Peter's courage failed and he denied his Lord three times.

However, knowing the failures of the great men and women of the Bible must not encourage us to aim lower. To believe the pernicious lie that the unconditional love of God moves him to wink at deliberate sin and refuse to discipline his children is to ignore the fact that his discipline is evidence of his love (Heb. 12:4–6). God's love doesn't change, but our enjoyment of that love does change if we deliberately rebel against him. He wants to be a Father to us and to share his love and his wealth, but there are conditions attached (2 Cor. 6:14–7:1). Wasn't that what the prodigal son discovered in the far country (Luke 15:17–20)? Isn't it the kindness of God, not the badness of sin, that brings people to repentance (Rom. 2:4)?

If you are going to preach the Bible, you must learn to deal with occasional ambiguity, especially in the lives of Bible characters. "There was a time when I used to be troubled a good deal about these Bible characters," said evangelist D. L. Moody. "I used to think that, because they were saints, everything they did was right; and I could not understand just how it was that God would permit them to do such things and not be punished."[5] Of course, Moody was a serious Bible student and knew that the record of the Old Testament believers was given to warn us to turn from sin (1 Cor. 10:1–13), to encourage us and give us hope (Rom. 15:1–6), and to increase our faith (Hebrews 11). God did discipline his people for the wrongs they committed (2 Samuel 12; Ps. 99:8), but God still continued to use most of them to accomplish his divine will.

God still says, "Be holy because I, the LORD your God, am holy" (Lev. 19:2; 1 Peter 1:15), and "Be perfect, therefore, as your heavenly Father is perfect" (Matt. 5:48). He also provides the means by which we can avoid rebellion and deliberate disobedience. We have the interceding Son of God, the indwelling Spirit of God, the inspired Word of God, and our identification with Christ in his death, burial, and resurrection. If we lived under the law, we would ultimately give up on ourselves and everybody else, but since we live under God's grace, *we never give up on anybody!* Having the right attitude toward the people *to whom* you preach is just as important as having the right approach to the people *about whom* you preach. Andrew W. Blackwood used to caution preachers, "The minister should look upon the people locally as an opportunity, not as a problem."[6]

The seventeenth-century prelate Thomas Fuller summarizes this entire discussion in one pithy sentence: "Read not Books alone, but Man also, and chiefly Thyself."

4

BIOGRAPHICAL PREACHING DEMANDS THOROUGH PREPARATION[1]

In Joseph Heller's novel *Good As Gold,* a White House staff member makes the statement, "We're going to tell the truth, even if we have to lie about it." But Christian preachers don't do evil that good may come from it. We study, meditate, pray, and dig into the texts until we've reached that vein of truth that we can mine and mint for our people. (For this metaphor, see Proverbs 2:1–9, and take it to heart!) In conference workshops, I've told pastors to remember the "T POT" rule—"Take Plenty of Time." There are no exceptions to this rule. Trust me.

On March 25, 1842, Henry David Thoreau wrote in his journal, "Great persons are not soon learned, not even their outlines, but they change like the mountains on the horizon as we ride along." If you're preaching about Joseph, Moses, or Paul, you may gather more material than you need, even if you plan to do a series. You still must take time to narrow things down and focus on the approach for each message, because each message in a series must be able to stand alone. However, if you're preaching about Paul's nephew (Acts 23:11ff) or Simon the Zealot, you'll have to dig for material and will need extra time to probe deeper. It's embarrassing to preach on a Bible character and after the service have one of your listeners point out an important text you completely overlooked. It cannot be emphasized too much: take time to research the individual and gather the important factual data. T POT—Take Plenty of Time.

Gathering Material

What kind of information should we gather for the biographical sermon? Everything that's available and useful to our purpose, the kind of information we'd need for writing a biography. This would include family background, vocation, education and training (there is a difference), early influences, important people in his or her life, crisis experiences, important decisions, evidences of change, and maturity. Be sure to include the New Testament texts that deal with Old Testament characters. Your complete concordance will assist you here. I like to take notes on 3 x 4 pieces of paper. I write a topical heading on each note and the text to which it applies. If it's a quotation, I add the documentation. When my search for data is ended, I can arrange the notes topically (birth, family, name, etc.) and have an easier time seeing what I have to work with. Some of the notes will end up in the wastebasket or perhaps be filed away for a future message.

Start with a chronology of the character's life and a listing of contemporaries, and then start asking yourself questions. If you're dealing with a person from the Gospels, be sure to have your harmony of the Gospels handy. When I did a series on John the Baptist, my preparation included making a photocopy of every passage in the Gospels that related to him and putting the sheets into a binder. What a time-saver that proved to be!

This is the kind of material you're searching for:

Anything unique in the person's birth or death? Check any available genealogies. Remember that some names are repeated often in Scripture, so don't confuse the Herods, Marys, and Zechariahs.

Is the person's name significant? Was the name ever changed? Any nicknames?

What did the person most enjoy? trust? do? fail in? succeed in? Can you find high points and low points?

How did the person respond to God's Word? to other people? to danger? to failure? to success? to God's will?

How did the person influence other people, for good or for ill? What were his or her lasting achievements? What are the person's influences today?

If the person spoke or wrote anything that is recorded in Scripture, what do the words reveal about his or her life? We can learn a great deal about Simon Peter from his two epistles. Several Old Testament persons are named in the Psalms and some in the Prophets.

What geographical information is important?

How would this person fit into society today? Into the church? Would I want him or her as a friend? a neighbor? a co-laborer for Christ?

What part did this person play in the salvation history recorded in the Bible?

Do I know anybody who is like this person? In what ways am I like him or her?

What great truth, if any, does this life illustrate? What familiar metaphor or proverb would fit this person?

You need not include every piece of information in your sermon, but learn all you can about your subject and carefully weigh each facet of his or her personality. Don't try to be a sanctified amateur psychiatrist, but do try to enter into the person's heart, mind, and circumstances. Otherwise, your message will be only the story of a person's life, a biographical lecture without any interpretation, insight, or application. This doesn't mean that we turn the life into an allegory, although we must identify the Old Testament types of Jesus Christ (e.g., Jonah, David, Joseph, etc.). The key question is, How did God work in and through this person to accomplish his will and glorify his name? (See John 17:4.)

Whether you have a great deal of data or very little, beware of an overactive imagination that "fills in the gaps" with extrabiblical ideas. There is a right way and a wrong way to fill in the gaps, and two examples from Charles Spurgeon will illustrate them. The first one is taken from Matthew 9:9 and shows a right way to do it.

> Matthew wrote this verse about himself. I can fancy him, with his pen in his hand, writing all the rest of this Gospel; but I can imagine that, when he came to this very personal passage, he laid the pen down a minute, and wiped his eyes.[2]

What Spurgeon described *could* have happened—it's true to human nature—and it *may* have happened, but he was careful not to say that it *did* happen. It happened only in the preacher's imagination and touched his heart, so he passed it along to his congregation and no doubt touched the hearts of many of them. But, like many of us, Mr. Spurgeon sometimes let his imagination get out of hand. The text is Matthew 27:19, the message Pilate received from his wife during the trial of Jesus.

> In her dream Pilate's wife may have seen her husband brought forth to judgment, himself a prisoner to be tried by the Just One, who had earlier been accused before him. She may have awoke, startled at the shriek of her husband as he fell back into the pit that knows no bottom.[3]

There was a time when this kind of pulpit oratory was expected and appreciated, but fortunately that era ended long ago, except in small pockets of the church where oratory is protected by tradition. Spurgeon didn't know the contents of the woman's dream or why it made her suffer. Human speculation is no substitute for divine revelation.

Look for a Key

"All persons are puzzles until at last we find in some word or act the key to the man, to the woman," wrote Ralph Waldo Emerson; "straightway all their past words and actions lie in light before us."[4]

This is not likely to be some unusual thing but something common to humanity in general. "The men of the Bible Gallery are photographed because they are *universal* men," said George Matheson.[5] An understanding of human nature begins with an understanding of our own hearts, an experience that can be painful.

I've long thought that Psalm 78:70–72 provides one key to David's life: David the shepherd, the man with integrity in his heart and skill in his hands. Psalm 78 describes the sins and failures of the people of Israel and how God dealt with them; but the solution to the nation's problems was a new leader, a shepherd who was a man after God's own heart. David saw himself as the shepherd of the people and he sought to protect them (2 Sam. 24:17). Frequently when you find King Saul in Scripture, his spear is mentioned, the proud emblem of his authority. But in his hand David had a sling, a sword, a harp, a cup of cold water (2 Sam. 23:13–17), and a pen (2 Sam. 11:12–17). He had nothing in his hand when he confessed his sins (Ps. 51:16–17). Another image of Saul is that of the king standing head and shoulders above everybody else at the beginning of his career (1 Sam. 10:23) and then at the end falling on his face (1 Sam. 28:14) and on his sword (1 Sam. 31:1–4). "How the mighty have fallen!" lamented David when he heard the news (2 Sam. 1:25, 27). Saul's pride led him into sin, so Proverbs 16:18 would also apply.

One key to the life of Mary of Bethany is that Scripture pictures her at the feet of Jesus (Luke 10:38–42; John 11:32; 12:1–8). Andrew the apostle is introduced as a man who brought people to Jesus (John 1:35–42; 6:1–9; 12:20–22). Nicodemus is identified with the night (John 3:1–2; 19:38–42), but he came out of the darkness and into the light. Judas, on the other hand, went out into the night (John 13:30). In John's writings, darkness symbolizes sin, Satan, and spiritual ignorance. Nicodemus illustrates John 3:19–21.

Surely John 3:30 is a key to the life and ministry of John the Baptist: "He must become greater; I must become less." Jesus was the bridegroom and John was only the best man (John 3:29). Jesus is the Word, but John was only a voice (John 1:23). Jesus is the light (John 8:12), but John was only a lamp (John 5:35). John was filled with the Spirit before birth and therefore rejoiced in Jesus and glorified Jesus.

The Greek biographer Plutarch (c. AD 46–119), whose *Lives of the Noble Grecians and Romans* is still read today, made an astute observation that can help us in our biographical studies. "And the most glorious exploits do not always furnish us with the clearest discoveries of virtue and vice in men; sometimes a matter of less moment, an expression or a jest, informs us better of their characters and inclinations, than the most famous sieges, the greatest armaments, or the bloodiest battles whatsoever."[6]

Package the Material Creatively

The easiest approach to the biographical sermon is chronological, but it isn't terribly interesting, unless you do a dramatic monologue. Merely discussing the stages in a person's life doesn't convey spiritual truth forcefully unless your development of each point is meaningful. For example:

Judas the disciple (Luke 6:12–13a)
Judas the apostle (Luke 6:13b–16)
Judas the devil (John 6:68–71)
Judas the thief (John 12:6)
Judas the defiled (John 13:10–11)
Judas the traitor (John 13:21–30; Acts 1:16)
Judas the suicide (Matt. 27:3–10)
Judas the son of destruction (John 17:12)
Judas the man who was better off unborn (Matt. 26:24)

Before he was chosen to become an apostle, Judas was in the large crowd of disciples that followed Jesus (Matt. 5:25), but why was he following the Lord? Was he hoping for the restoration of the Jewish kingdom? Was he fascinated by the miracles? *You can be in the crowd and not be in God's family!* Then he was called to be an apostle. *You can be a member of the inner circle and be a devil!* How did Judas respond when he heard the Sermon on the Mount, especially Matthew 7:21–27? *You can be at the table with the Lord and still surrender to the devil!* Judas is certainly a warning to every religious person who masquerades as a child of God. At this point you may want to study the parable of the tares (Matt. 13:24–30, 36–43).

The title "the one doomed to destruction" (John 17:12) could be one key to Judas's tragic life, for the word *apoleia* (destruction) is translated "waste" in Matthew 26:8 and Mark 14:4, where Judas and the other disciples ask, "Why this waste?" Judas was "the son of the wasteness." He certainly wasted a glorious opportunity to be saved and to know and serve Jesus. He wasted a good name—Judah, which means "praise." His life ended in waste and he left a cemetery behind. To be sure, Judas is one of the most enigmatic of all the personalities in the Bible, yet we must try to make something out of his life and death. Jesus gave Judas power to do miracles and the responsibility to preach sermons (Luke 9:1–6), and he was apparently successful, for the other disciples never once questioned his right to be among them. They did not know there was a traitor among them until the very end. These are certainly deep waters.

Instead of merely tracing a person's life, we might focus on the crises in his or her life or the lessons learned from the Lord. Jonah learned the lesson of God's presence (chap. 1), God's pardon (chap. 2), God's power (chap. 3), and God's pity (chap. 4). We aren't told how the story ended, but we certainly discover that you can't run away from the Lord, that the Lord does forgive us and deigns to use us, and that his heart is broken by the sins of the people who need to hear our message. But our own sin keeps us from telling the message!

Each biographical sermon must be controlled by both the text(s) and a compelling purpose. We must know what the message is supposed to accomplish in the lives of the hearers. According to 2 Timothy 3:1, the Word of God should teach us doctrine, reprove sin, correct our lives, and show us how to keep our lives in God's will; merely recounting a person's life may not be enough. Yes, the Spirit can use the story to speak to hearts, but the Spirit was given to glorify the Son of God (John 16:14), so don't leave Jesus out of the message. I have heard sermons by capable preachers in which Jesus was never mentioned, and this, I think, is a mistake.

5

PREACHING A
BIOGRAPHICAL SERIES

You have several approaches from which to choose when preparing to preach a biographical series. You could do a longer series on a Bible character such as Abraham, Moses, King Saul, David, Peter, or Paul, but don't let the series go too long. Highlight the important events and experiences and leave the interesting details for another time. Each individual message must be complete and meaningful to the listener who hasn't heard the entire series. If you want to alienate sporadic attendees and occasional visitors, start each message with, "You will recall that three weeks ago we found David in a cave." They weren't in church three weeks ago, so they conclude that they won't get much out of the latest message.

There should be a theme for the series that ties the messages together and holds the interest of the congregation. Alan Redpath's series on David preached at Moody Church—*The Making of a Man of God*—is an excellent example of a series controlled by an important theme. Each sermon has its own development and helps to explain how God molded David into an effective leader. A similar approach could be used for Moses or Peter. But you need not cover the person's entire life; you can be selective. I enjoyed doing a series on the miracles in the life of Peter,[1] and another on the crises that led to the fall of King Saul ("Don't Lose Your Crown").

A second approach is to select several individuals who are linked by an important theme. A number of people in the Bible said "I have sinned," and some of them meant it. This makes an interesting series, although Spurgeon put seven of them into one message, a remarkable feat for a preacher only twenty-two years old.[2] I once used this theme as a Lenten series. A theme such as "Great Affirmations of Faith" offers an opportunity to challenge the people to take their stand and do what is right. Consider Job (13:15), Ruth (1:16–18), the prophet Habakkuk (chap. 3), Peter (Matt. 16:13–20), the thief on the cross (Luke 23:33–43), and the apostle Paul (2 Tim. 1:8–12). Again, I refer you to the sermon books of Clarence Edward Macartney and Clovis Chappell, both of whom knew how to find the links that bound Bible biographies together.

A third approach is to borrow an idea from F. W. Boreham and deal with the verses that "belonged" to great personalities in church history and in literature.[3] In your daily Bible reading or in your sermon preparation, you might come across a text that sheds light on the character you are studying. For example, when I read Proverbs 28:13 I suddenly realized, *Why, this text perfectly fits David!* Later I also saw the connection between this passage and 1 John 1:5–10. Likewise, if you compare Acts 9:3; 22:6; and 26:13, you will see how Proverbs 4:18 applies to Paul's life.

One final word: preach about the notable women of the Bible as well as the notable men. There's a trend today to preach about the "bad girls of the Bible," which is fine *if you magnify God's grace and not the women's sins.* Esther helps us better understand the will of God and the providence of God (especially 4:10–17); and before she became a sinner, Eve certainly pictures the ideal woman. In fact, using Eve as the key person, you can do a series of three messages on (1) what the woman ought to be, (2) what marriage ought to be, and (3) what the church ought to be (Eph. 5:18–33). Jesus admonished us to "remember Lot's wife" (Luke 17:26–33), and Moses advised us to "remember Miriam" (Deut. 24:9). Both Isaac's wife Rebekah and Samuel's mother Hannah are choice personalities for sermon series, and no doubt you will see that Mary, the mother of Jesus, was familiar with Hannah's song. Of course, King Ahab's evil wife Jezebel is a woman whose deeds are so reprehensible that you marvel at the long-suffering of the Lord. But I hasten to remind you, don't major on the sin and neglect the Savior from sin.

Our primary source of information about Bible characters is, of course, the Bible, but if you have the time, investigate what great literature has to say about them. *A Dictionary of Biblical Tradition in English Literature,* edited by David Lyle Jeffery (Grand Rapids: Eerdmans, 1992), can direct you to many literary treatments of Bible personalities. *Chapters into Verse,* two volumes assembled and edited by Robert Atwan and Laurence Wilder (Oxford, 1993), will give you the actual poems along with the Scripture verses on which they are based. However, not all your listeners will have an appetite for these literary treasures, and some will think you are "liberal" for using them, so handle with care. I find that a gifted poet can often bring out a point that I missed in my Bible research, so let's be grateful for all the help we can get!

PART 2

RESOURCES
FOR THE
BIOGRAPHICAL
SERMON

This anthology is a small sampling of the vast treasury of material available to assist you in biographical preaching and in your own spiritual walk. I haven't tried to cover all the people in the Bible or even all of those we would call important. The purpose of the anthology is not only to give you material but also to suggest what kind of material is available. Whatever gives us insight into character and how people either build or destroy it is valuable to us. The bibliography on page 203 will help you add some of the best books to your library; of course, you should never buy a book unless it's the kind of tool you can really use. I have not mentioned some of the more contemporary books on Bible characters because you can examine them in the bookstore or check them out online and in catalogs. Instead, this bibliography helps you "re-dig the old wells" and find treasures in places you may have neglected.

Following is an explanation of some abbreviations I have used in the documentation. Full publication facts are given in the bibliography. Items not documented are taken from that vast public domain file that has been around for many years and is often attributed to "Anonymous" or "Selected."

AW-BC   Alexander Whyte, *Bible Characters from the Old and New Testaments*

CEM   Clarence Edward Macartney, various volumes of sermons

CHS   Charles Haddon Spurgeon, *The Metropolitan Tabernacle Pulpit* (CHS, 14:349 would refer to volume 14, page 349)

GCM   G. Campbell Morgan, *The Westminster Pulpit* (unless otherwise identified)

GHM   George H. Morrison, various volumes of sermons

GM-RMB   George Matheson, *The Representative Men of the Bible*

GM-RWB   George Matheson, *The Representative Women of the Bible*

WWW   Material from my own preaching and writing. If somebody else's material has crept in and I have claimed it, I apologize. If you can document the source for me, I would appreciate it.

A

Aaron

Aaron's light is dimmed by the brighter light of Moses, his brother, to such an extent that many fail to catch the full stature of the man and of his ministry. The lesser lights fare badly in the presence of the greater—the moon before the sun.

A. T. Robertson, Passing On the Torch, p. 52

[Exodus 17:8–16] Moses did the praying and Joshua did the fighting. Aaron and Hur performed the humble task of holding up the hands of Moses in prayer.

A. T. Robertson, Passing On the Torch, p. 54

[Exodus 32:1ff] Here was Aaron's great opportunity such as comes to many a man once. If eloquence was ever needed, it was now. But, like many a preacher or politician since that day, Aaron temporized with the people and encouraged their restless doubt. He became a follower of the rabble, instead of becoming the leader of the multitude. He put his ear to the ground to hear the rumblings of the groundling instead of lifting up his voice to sound a bugle note of loyalty to God.

A. T. Robertson, Passing On the Torch, p. 56

[Exodus 32:1–6] "Up, make us gods, which shall go before us. . . ."
They were abandoning Jehovah, and placing themselves under the
conduct of manufactured gods—gods of man's making. . . . Alas!
alas! it has ever been thus in man's history. The human heart loves
something that can be seen; it loves that which meets and gratifies
the senses. It is only faith that can "endure as seeing him who is
invisible." Hence, in every age, men have been forward to set up
and lean upon human imitations of divine realities.

C. H. Mackintosh, *Notes on the Book of Exodus,* p. 356

[Exodus 32:24] Like all timid men, [Aaron] trembled before the
storm which he had raised. And so he tried to persuade Moses,
and perhaps in some degree even to persuade himself, that it
was not he that had done this thing. He lays the blame upon the
furnace. . . . We are all ready to lay the blame upon the furnaces.
"The fire did it," we are all of us ready enough to say.

Phillips Brooks, "The Fire and the Calf,"
in *Sermons Preached in English Churches,* pp. 44–45

[On Aaron's excuse:] Everywhere there is this cowardly casting off
of responsibilities upon the dead circumstances around us.

Brooks, "The Fire and the Calf," p. 49

All went well with Aaron as long as he had Moses beside him
to inspire him, and to support him, and to be to him instead of
God. . . . But always when Moses was for any length of time out
of sight, Aaron was a reed shaken with the wind; he was as weak
and as evil as any other man. Those forty days that Moses was
away on the Mount brought out, among other things, both Moses'
strength and greatness and Aaron's littleness and weakness in a
way that nothing else could have done.

AW-BC, p. 127

Put enough gold trinkets together and you have an idol!

An excuse is the skin of a reason stuffed with a lie.

I have always regarded him [Aaron] as the Simon Peter of the Old Testament.

GM-RMB, 2:92

Moses is shy; Aaron is bold. Moses is reticent; Aaron is outspoken. Moses halts in utterance; Aaron is a man of eloquence. Moses is meek and prone to wait the tide of events; Aaron is an impetuous spirit and tends to rush into action. Moses meditates forty years in the desert of Midian; Aaron in that same desert seems to have been doing powerful service in winning the favor of the neighboring chiefs. And yet the fact remains that Moses was the chosen man, the man selected to be the leader of the rising age. Why is this? . . . It lies in the fact that the Bible has a different estimate of strength from that made by the secular eye.

GM-RMB, 2:88–89

Aaron and Hur (Exodus 17:8–16)

I wish that some of our pastors were sustained as they should be by their Aarons and their Hurs. Alas, I know many a fainting brother whose hands are hanging down, who finds an Aaron to pull them lower still, and a Hur to depress his spirits more.

CHS, 12:538

Abel

New Testament references: Matthew 23:35; Luke 11:51; Hebrews 11:4; 12:24; 1 John 3:12.

When the heart believes, the mouth follows suit and makes confession. Faith made Noah a preacher, and it caused it to be said of Abel, "He being dead yet speaketh."

CHS, 26:618

Abraham

See Matthew 1:1; Luke 13:16; 19:9; John 8:37–40; 8:56; Romans 4; Galatians 3:7–9, 29; James 2:21.

There are men who are before their time. They stand upon a hill and see the other side. They narrowly miss being heralds of the future. They only miss that destiny because their age is not ripe for them. Like Paul, they are "born out of due time"—born too soon. They have an Easter vision while it is yet winter. . . . They are in advance of their age, and therefore they are the victims of their age. They are ever the men of sacrifice. Such a man is Abraham.

GM-RMB, 1:111

Queen Victoria was out for a drive with Lady Errol, one of her ladies in waiting. Wanting to cheer her up—she still mourned the loss of Albert—Lady Errol said, "Oh, Your Majesty, think of when we shall see our dear ones again in heaven!" The Queen simply said, "Yes." Lady Errol said, "We will all meet in Abraham's bosom." The Queen replied, "I will *not* meet Abraham."

Adapted from *The Oxford Book of Royal Anecdotes*, p. 400

The God of glory appeared to our father Abraham.

Acts 7:2

God will not force you into acquiescence; there must be faith to answer when He calls. To hear Him amid our trials, that is faith; to hear Him amid our questionings is faith; to hear His voice in such an age as this is possible to faith and faith alone.

GHM, *Morning Sermons,* p. 147

Abraham was not elected for his own sake merely. He was elected for the sake of others.

GHM, *Morning Sermons,* p. 142

[Hebrews 11:8] It is always a travesty of true religion when it withdraws a man from duty. The pilgrim spirit means a loose hold of much, but it never means a light and heedless heart.

GHM, *Morning Sermons,* p. 153

Let a man aim at anything less than God, and he is always liable
to disappointment. . . . It is not by aiming too high that men are
baffled. They are baffled when they aim too low.

GHM, *Morning Sermons,* p. 155

God does not let us see where we are going. The all-important
thing is the direction. If moment by moment we are true to Him,
the Land of Promise may be left in His hands.

GHM, *Morning Sermons,* p. 158

Life is not raised above the stormy waters like some new island
by the shock of an earthquake. Life is built as is the coral island,
by infinitesimal toiling in the deeps, till it is raised into a thing of
beauty where beyond the breakers there is peace.

GHM, *Morning Sermons,* p. 208

Faith is not believing in spite of evidence. Faith is obeying in spite
of consequence.

G. A. Studdart-Kennedy

[Hebrews 11:8–19] By faith, Abraham obeyed when he did not
know *where* he was going (vv. 8–10), *how* the son would be born
(vv. 11–12), *when* the son would be born (vv. 13–16) and *why* he
had to sacrifice the son whom God gave him (vv. 17–19). He did
not know where, how, when or why—but he did know *Who.* The
important questions of life are answered, not by explanations, but
by promises, and those promises come from God.

[Genesis 20] There are no surprises of sin in holy lives. . . .
Abraham erred whenever he began to ask himself the question,
"What is now the safe and expedient course for me? What is
politic in the circumstances? What will make for my present
advantage?" He never erred when he asked himself, "What is
God's will?"

James Strahan, *Hebrew Ideals in Genesis,* pp. 139–40

A bad man's example has little influence over good men. But the
bad example of a good man, eminent in station and established
in reputation, has an enormous power for evil.

Strahan, *Hebrew Ideals,* p. 141

[Genesis 22] The bitterest struggles in this life are not always
the struggles between right and wrong. Sometimes the bitterest
struggles of the soul are the conflicts between right and right.

GHM, *Morning Sermons,* p. 232

To obey God then, as now, meant often, if not always, to disobey
men. To please God meant then, as now, to displease yourself and
your neighbors and the devil, and to make things very unpleasant
all round in a general sort of way. . . . There are not two standards
of service—one a painful one for Abraham and the other an easy
one for you.

General William Booth, *Salvation Soldiery,* pp. 98–99

You admire Abraham's giving up his son to God. Much more
admire Jehovah's giving up His Son for sinners.

CHS, 29:437

God was a great deal more tender with Abraham than He was with
Himself. When His own Son was dying upon a cross on that very
same mountain, He didn't send a victim to take His place, but left
Him there to die, the just for the unjust, that He might redeem us
and bring us back to God.

D. L. Moody, in *Moody: His Words, Work, and Workers,* p. 152

[Genesis 25:8] Abraham was "full of years," or "satisfied with life."
He had seen, felt, labored, loved, suffered enough; he knew all the
contents of time; earth had no more to offer him—and so the years
brought him a sense of completeness. Ripened by divine grace,
satisfied but not sated, enjoying life to the last, yet willing to let it
go—that is how we picture an aged servant of God.

Strahan, *Hebrew Ideals,* p. 197

[The Hebrews] believed that righteousness lengthened life and glorified it at the end. See Proverbs 16:31; Psalms 34:12–14; 92:14; Job 11:17; Isaiah 46:4; Zechariah 14:7.

Strahan, *Hebrew Ideals, p.* 198

Achan

The Valley of Achor ("trouble, disaster") is referred to in Joshua 7:24–26; 15:7; Isaiah 65:10; Hosea 2:15.

But war is war, and the best of commanders cannot make war a silken work, nor can he hold down the devil in the hearts of his men.

AW-BC, p. 172

The beginning of all temptations is inconstancy of mind and small confidence in God. . . . For first there comes to the mind a bare thought of evil, then a strong imagination thereof, afterwards delight, and an evil motion [a small concession], and then consent.

Thomas à Kempis, *The Imitation of Christ,* 1.13.5

Adam

O merciful God, grant that the old Adam in this child may be so buried, that the new man may be raised in him.

"Baptism of Infants," from *The Book of Common Prayer*

Saints are so righteous in Jesus Christ that they are more righteous than Adam was before he fell, for he had but a creature righteousness and they have the righteousness of the Creator.

CHS, 28:536

There was nothing in the whole Garden of Eden that could give Adam a moment's delight, because he was under a sense of sin. And so will it be with you. If you could be put in paradise, you would not be happier.

CHS, 6:216

This venture of God in which he bound himself to man—and exposed himself to the possibility of being reviled, despised, denied, and ignored by man—this venture was the first flash of his love. God ventured, as it were, his own self. . . . This line reaches its end in Jesus Christ.

Helmut Thielicke, How the World Began, pp. 60–61

There is no ancient gentlemen but gardeners, ditchers and gravemakers; they hold up Adam's profession.

Shakespeare, Hamlet, 5.1.44

Agrippa (Acts 26:28)

Almost persuaded to be a Christian is like the man who was almost pardoned, but he was hanged; like the man who was almost rescued, but he was burned in the house. A man who is almost saved is damned.

CHS, 14:427

Ahab

There is a familiar saying, "Every man has his price." Ahab had his price, and he sold himself for a garden!

Ananias (Acts 9:10–19)

We hear of him this once and we know nothing more about him. He comes forward at a critical point in Paul's life, executes for him a very useful office, and then disappears. The good soldier was sent upon a special service by his Captain, and when he had fulfilled his commission he returned to his ordinary place in the ranks.

CHS, 31:242

He did not ask, "What for?" but said "Here am I," ready for anything.

CHS, 31:245

The Lord knows the street and he knows the house where the
sinner lives who is to be blessed by you.

CHS, 31:246

Go ye, then, my brethren and sisters, wherever God sends you;
for you know not what may be within a man, a woman, or a child
whom you shall bring to Jesus. Everybody is not a Paul, but yet
you may find a Paul among your converts.

CHS, 31:252

Ananias and Sapphira (Acts 5)

There have been successors to Ananias and Sapphira as well as
to the apostles.

GCM, 5:31

Andrew

Andrew is found three times in the Gospel of John, and each
reference shows him bringing people to Jesus (1:35–42; 6:1–14;
12:20–26).

Charles Spurgeon refers to Andrew as "the missionary disciple."

CHS, 15:86

Bringing Peter to Christ

Andrew was earnest for the souls of others, though he was but *a
young convert.* So far as I can gather, he appeared to have beheld
Jesus as the Lamb of God one day, and to have found out his
brother Peter the next.

CHS, 15:87

Andrew was . . . a man of average capacity. He was not at all the
brilliant character that Simon Peter his brother turned out to be.

CHS, 15:88

Andrew proved his wisdom in that *he set great store by a single soul.*
. . . What a task for the arithmetician, to value one soul! One soul
sets all heaven's bells ringing by its repentance. One sinner that
repenteth maketh angels rejoice.

CHS, 15:94

Andrew is regularly described and identified as Simon Peter's
brother (Matt. 10:2; Luke 6:14; John 6:8). The inference is that
people might not know who Andrew was, but everyone knew who
Peter was, and the best way to identify Andrew was to call him the
brother of the famous and outstanding Peter. There are very few
people in Andrew's position who could have borne that situation
with graciousness and without resentment. . . . But Andrew was
one of those people who did not care who received the first place.
All he wanted was to be near to Jesus.

William Barclay, *The Master's Men*, p. 41

The crying need is for Andrews, men of conviction, men of faith,
men who believe enough about Jesus Christ to make it worthwhile
to tell others, and men who do tell others, who do bring others,
who do seek to act for Christ.

CEM, *He Chose Twelve*, p. 18

The "Inner Circle"

Jesus had His "inner circle" composed of Peter, James, and John.
They went with Him to the Mount of Transfiguration (Matt. 17:1–
13), into the home of Jairus (Luke 8:49–56), and into the Garden
of Gethsemane (Mark 14:32–42). These three events parallel Philippians 3:10.

WWW

It never troubled Andrew that he was not among the first three. It
never distressed him that men talked more of Peter and James and
John than they did of him. All Andrew thought of was *the work.*

J. D. Jones, *The Glorious Company of Apostles,* p. 96

[Note: J. D. Jones compared Andrew to the Old Testament soldier Benaiah, one of David's "mighty men," who did not attain to the status of the first three warriors (1 Chron. 11:22–25).]

Every country is renewed out of the unknown ranks and not out of the ranks of those already famous and powerful and in control.

President Woodrow Wilson, October 28, 1912

We may often know much about a man if we know his friends. We look at the friends of Andrew. John the Baptist was one, and John the apostle was another.

His name Andrew, Andreas, means "manly."

GCM, *The Great Physician,* p. 19

Christ's first disciple was not Peter, but Andrew, and the first need of the Lord is still the strong, quiet soul who is content to remain largely out of sight.

GCM, *The Great Physician,* p. 24

No man can become a living follower of the Lord without immediately finding His compassion moving him, and driving him out after someone else.

GCM, *The Great Physician,* p. 23

[T]he last place in which the name of Andrew is revealed is on one of the foundation stones of the city of God (Rev. 21:14). . . . I am constrained to say that as you look at that city, you will find that Simon had no greater or more conspicuous stone than had Andrew . . . the building of the city of God will not be accomplished because of the notoriety of its builders, but because of their fidelity.

GCM, *The Great Physician,* pp. 23–24

In the calendar of the Anglican Church, St. Andrew's Day is November 30th. This is also the birthdate of Mark Twain (1835) and Sir Winston Churchill (1874). On November 30, 1864, missionaries John Clough and his wife sailed for India where he preached the Gospel and many were converted. He and two Indian preachers baptized 2,222 converts in one day, and the baptisms continued for two more days. Andrew would have been overjoyed.

WWW

The Last We Hear of Andrew in the Gospels, He Is Listening to the Word

Andrew appears only once more by name in the Gospels. It is on the Mount of Olives after Jesus had . . . foretold the destruction of the wonderful building of whose beauty they had spoken to Jesus (Mark 13:3ff).

A. T. Robertson, *Some Minor Characters in the New Testament,*
pp. 22–23

In Acts 1, we find Andrew praying. In Acts 2, he is listening to his brother preach! He is still in second place and enjoying it.

WWW

B

Balaam

He was the solitary self-seeker—alone, isolated, loving to be separated from all other men; admired, feared and sought.

F. W Robertson, *Sermons,* 4:37

Balaam asks permission of God again. Here is the evidence of a secret hollowness in his heart, however fair the outside seemed. In worldly matters "think twice"; but in duty, it has well been said, "first thoughts are best." . . . Deliberation is often dishonesty. God's guidance is plain, when we are true. . . . "With the froward"—oh how true!—"thou wilt show thyself froward." [See also Ps. 18:26.]

F. W. Robertson, *Sermons,* 4:38–39

Balaam did what men so entangled always do. The real fault is in themselves. They have committed themselves to a false position, and when obstacles stand in their way, they lay the blame on circumstances.

F. W. Robertson, *Sermons,* 4:40

Balaam wanted to please himself without displeasing God.

F. W. Robertson, *Sermons,* 4:42

God will not curse the good; therefore, Balaam tries to make them wicked; he tries to make the good curse themselves, and so exasperate God. [Num. 25; 31:15–16; Rev. 2:14]

F. W. Robertson, *Sermons,* 4:47

See how a man may be going on uttering fine words, orthodox truths, and yet be rotten at heart.

F. W. Robertson, *Sermons,* 4:50

If we want to die the death of the righteous, we had better live the life of the righteous!

Balaam's insidious device for getting his own way while pretending to seek God's will was simply *to get a different perspective.* Keep looking for a "different angle" and you will probably find one, and wish you hadn't.

WWW

Barnabas

Thus we see that Barnabas staked his all—his reputation, his life, his church which was dearer than life—on Paul's sincerity. He gave Saul the weight of his influence, which weight was like a mighty anchor to a ship tempest beaten. He gave his hand, which hand was like a keen sword to one sorely pressed in battle. Had it not been for that warm and strong extended hand of Barnabas, Saul might have been chilled into obscurity. . . .

R. G. Lee, *Glory Today for Conquest Tomorrow,* p. 89

Barnabas played second fiddle, but he played it so well that the Kingdom of God made progress. He rode second in the Gospel chariot, but he did it with such humility and joy and gratitude until heaven will forever rejoice that he was "a good man, full of the Holy Ghost and of faith" and that, because of him, "much people were added to the Lord" [Acts 11:24].

Lee, *Glory Today,* p. 96

When Paul had gone back to Tarsus and Barnabas had gone to electrify with his wisdom the Church at Antioch, the older preacher was sad because he had all the glory. He wanted the young man to share it; he determined that he should share it. He went to Tarsus and brought him to the scene of triumph. He gave him a place among the Christian workers. He went about continually in his company, that men might say, "There go Barnabas and [Saul]." He knew well the power of association—how a tarnished name if linked with a great name may lose its tarnish; and he resolved that Paul should reap the advantage of such a union.

GM-RMB, 2:298

Baruch (Jer. 45:45)

There in a flash we have the revelation of the difference between true and false ambition. That reveals the peril of ambition. When the whole is lost sight of and its well-being is not sought, ambition becomes deadly. The action growing out of it becomes cruel and ruthless. When a man seeks great things for himself, what cares he how many suffer so that he succeeds; how many are downtrodden so that he may rise; how many are flung out by the whirling wheel, so long as he arrives at the goal? Such ambition is the spawn of hell, the "progeny" of Lucifer who fell from his high estate by ambition that was entirely self-centered.

GCM, 9:26

Boaz

The men of his day would have valued him for something impersonal. From a worldly point of view he had many advantages. He was of a good family. He had great social influence. He was possessed of much wealth. He belonged to a tribe which was already beginning to take the lead in Israel. But by none of these things does this man endure. Their remembrance is only kept alive by the remembrance of another quality, which his contemporaries would have passed by—the possession of a tender heart.

GM-RMB, 2:131

Boaz pictures Jesus Christ as Lord of the harvest and the one willing to sacrifice so that he might claim his bride. The unnamed kinsman redeemer would not forfeit his inheritance, but Boaz made Ruth a part of his inheritance!

WWW

C

Caiaphas

And see what he is! A crafty schemer, as blind as a mole to the beauty of Christ's character and the greatness of His words; utterly unspiritual; undisguisedly selfish; rude as a boor; cruel as a cut-throat; and having reached that supreme height of wickedness in which he can dress his ugliest thought in the plainest words, and send them into the world unabashed.

Alexander Maclaren, *Christ in the Heart*, p. 259

He can take one point of view only, in regard of the mightiest spiritual revelation that the world ever saw; and that is, its bearing upon his own miserable personal interests, and the interests of the order to which he belongs. And so whatever may be the wisdom, or miracles, or goodness of Jesus, because He threatens the prerogatives of the priesthood, He must die and be got out of the way. . . . Caiaphas' sin is possible, and Caiaphas' temptation is actual, for every man whose profession it is to handle the oracles of God.

Maclaren, *Christ in the Heart*, p. 260

Cain

Sin came into the world full-grown; the first man born of woman was a murderer.

D. L. Moody

Sin has entered into the world, and the happy innocence of Eden is destroyed. Cain is born, and the word Cain means possession; Abel is born, and the word Abel means vanity. Was it beginning to dawn thus early on mankind that "man at his best estate is altogether vanity" (Ps. 39:5 KJV)? The curse is beginning to work out to its fulfillment, and men are finding that the wages of sin is death.

GHM, *Footsteps of the Flock,* p. 16

So what does it mean, after all, that Cain should come to the altar? Our wicked heart is quite capable of devising mischief even in holy places, and as we sing hymns the wolves may be howling in the cellars of our souls.

Thielicke, *How the World Began,* p. 192

The history of the world is the space in which Cain's axe finally becomes dynamite and phosphorus, hydrogen explosions and space rockets.

Thielicke, *How the World Began,* p. 188

No, envy can be combated only by letting God give me a new faith, a faith that accepts the other person just as he has been sent to me by a higher hand, as someone who has his place and function in God's plan exactly as I have, as someone who confronts me with the command of love and in whom God's higher thoughts can come to me.

Thielicke, *How the World Began,* p. 197

Do not say, "Am I my brother's keeper?" for I shall have to give you a horrible answer if you do. I shall have to say, "No, Cain, you are not your brother's keeper but you are your brother's killer." If, by your effort you have not sought his good, by your neglect you have destroyed him.

CHS, 33:672

Not to love is to hate, and to hate is to kill. See 1 John 3:10–23.
                                                                    WWW

Caleb

He is "the man who wholly followed the Lord." God said it (Num. 14:24), Moses said it (Num. 32:12; Deut. 1:36), Joshua said it (Josh. 14:14), and Caleb said it himself (Josh. 14:8–9). He was wholehearted in his walk with the Lord.

As the ten faithless spies not only missed Canaan for themselves but caused tens of thousands of others to miss it, so the two faithful spies not only gained Canaan but they were used of God to lead that entire younger generation into their inheritance in the promised land.

Ruth Paxson, *Caleb the Overcomer*, p. 39

See Deuteronomy 1:35–36. With God, there are no "generation gaps." See also 2 Timothy 2:2 and Titus 2:1–8.

Give me men to match my mountains.

Inscription on the State Capitol, Sacramento, CA

Never measure the height of a mountain, until you have reached the top. Then you will see how low it was.

Dag Hammarskjöld, *Markings*, p. 7

It was not the great walled cities of Canaan nor even the great stature of the giants that kept them [Israel] from their inheritance in Canaan. It was their own faulty relationship to the Lord. [Numbers 13]

Paxson, *Caleb*, p. 28

The ten spies saw themselves primarily in relation to their enemies. Consequently their chief concern was for their safety. So they would sacrifice their inheritance in Canaan rather than risk their lives.

Paxson, *Caleb*, p. 32

During all the forty years of wilderness wandering, Caleb lived in the promised land through anticipatory appropriating faith. He lived *above* the wilderness by living *in* the promised land. He was *in* the wilderness, but not of it.

Paxson, Caleb, p. 51

What shall we do with life's mountains? We can climb them as did Moses and see the glory of God (Exod. 34). We can level them in the power of the Spirit (Zech. 4) and move ahead in our labors. We can exercise faith and trust the Lord to move them out of the way (Matt. 17:19–21). And, like Caleb, we can conquer them and claim them for our own inheritance.

WWW

Here is where many Christians fail. I haven't a question that many preachers largely fail because they are looking for easy and soft places. The one thing we are to think about, to care for, is that we may stand in the battle's front and in the thick of the fight, every man where God wants him, whether lawyer, doctor, minister, teacher, banker, farmer, or what not. If God has hard tasks and big jobs, and gigantic undertakings, let each one give himself to them with the spirit of Caleb, scorning easy places, asking for God to give him anything He wishes, in His infinite wisdom and love. . . . Let us address ourselves to life's problems as did Caleb. Let us make up our minds never to get old, never. Let us make up our minds that we will never admit for a breath to ourselves that suggestion of the devil, that we have "done our part."

George W. Truett, We Would See Jesus, p. 101

Caleb was a man who was perennially young. That is one of the most beautiful things in his life story. . . . There is not any place, there is not any need for any man ever to get old in this world. And if a man will link himself with the right things, and have the right viewpoint in the life he lives, he will never be an old man.

Truett, We Would See Jesus, p. 99

Caleb was a man who dared to be in the minority. He was a man who could, without any blanching of face, go against the crowd.

He was a man who had his anchorage thoroughly defined, and who adjusted himself in absolute obedience to the convictions his soul felt and knew to be right. He dared, therefore, to be in the minority.

Truett, We Would See Jesus, p. 96

Caleb followed the Lord universally, without dividing [his heart]; sincerely, without dissembling; cheerfully, without disputing; constantly, without declining.

CHS, 9:620

Cornelius (Acts 10:1–11:18)

Cornelius wasn't to be saved by his feelings, nor his efforts, nor his alms; he was to be saved by words—the words of Peter preaching Jesus Christ to him. By such words not only Cornelius and all his house, but all sinners everywhere, are to be brought into the kingdom of God. [See Acts 11:14.]

Moody, Words, Work, and Workers, p. 124

D

Damaris (Acts 17:34)

Damaris was an Athenian woman who heard Paul's message on Mars Hill, believed on Jesus, and, along with some believing men, joined with Paul. The accent in her name is on the first syllable. Because the name is not found in ancient documents, some students change it from Damaris ("gentle") to Damalis ("a heifer"), a term that was applied to Greek courtesans who catered to the men of wealth, but we have absolutely no evidence that Damaris was that kind of woman. Perhaps she was among the aristocratic God-fearers who heard Paul in the synagogue (Acts 17:17) and followed him to Mars Hill. The fact that Luke mentions her by name suggests that she was a woman of rank who was known to the believers who would read his book and that her life had been exemplary. Important women had been converted to Christ in Philippi (Acts 16:13–15), Thessalonica (Acts 17:1–4), and Berea (Acts 17:10–12), and now in Athens. The varied responses to the Gospel that occurred in Athens still occur today: some laugh, some delay, and some believe. Damaris believed.

WWW

We get the impression that she had a mind naturally inclined to high things. Perhaps she had been baffled with life's perplexities and disappointments. . . . It took courage and self-denial for her to come out on the side of Christ and of Paul. . . . How much the church of Christ owes to women like that! And how much it needs such women today! . . . Can any of those Stoics or Epicureans be named who invited Paul to preach to them that day on Mars Hill? Not one of them! But the name of Paul still lives, and the name of Damaris, who chose Christ and eternal life, still lives, and will live forever, because her name is written in the Lamb's Book of Life.

CEM, *Chariots of Fire*, pp. 24–25

Daniel

See Ezekiel 14:14, 20; 28:3.

The story of Daniel is fascinating because it reveals the possibilities of godliness in the midst of the circumstances of ungodliness.

GCM, 8:221

The one universal feature of the portrait is its answer to the question, "What is the quality most needed by a young man?" The Book of Daniel I regard as beyond all things the young man's guide-book—the only book which has deliberately pointed out the quality which is essential to the formation of character. . . . What is it? It is courage—the spirit of daring. . . . The peculiarity of this man's courage is that from beginning to end it was laid in an unpoetic scene. . . . It was hailed by no spectators, cheered by no plaudits, accompanied by no bands of music. No eye looked on but the eye of conscience, no voice said "Well done!" but the voice of duty.

GM-RMB, 2:333–35

To know God is courage, and it is peace; but above all, it is power.

James S. Stewart, *The Gates of New Life*, p. 73

According to Bishop J. C. Ryle, the secret of Daniel's character was his steady walk with God, his habit of prayer and his confidence in God.

J. C. Ryle, *The True Christian*, pp. 247–51

Oh! that our prayers could get beyond praying, till they got to agonizing. . . . Not till it comes to travail—not till then—may we expect to see much done.

CHS, 61:521

Daniel was himself a prophet, but he studied the inspired prophecies of Jeremiah. If such a man need read Scripture, how much more ought we! [See Daniel 9:1–2.]

CHS, 61:528

Consequences! Never mind the consequences; there wasn't any such word in his dictionary. When it came to a question of obeying the law of his God, he was going to obey, and let God take care of the consequences.

Moody, *Words, Work, and Workers,* p. 67

Oh, for a grand character to support one's religious determination!

CHS, 39:40

Under all dispensations there have been men of the class to which Daniel belongs. The antediluvian period produced an Enoch who "walked with God and was not, for God took him," and he, like Daniel, prophesied concerning the coming of the Lord. In the patriarchal period there was an Abraham who is called "the friend of God," with whom the Lord communed in a most peculiar [distinctive from others] manner. In the after days, under the law, was there not a David, "a man after God's own heart"? . . . I might say that Daniel was the John of the prophets, and that John was the Daniel of the evangelists.

CHS, 19:1–2

Though he had been made a president of the empire, yet he was still a Jew; he felt himself still one with the seed of Israel. . . . [He] would remember them and pray for them, and would plead that their desolation might yet be removed. [See Daniel 9:19.]

CHS, 61:517

David

Two helpful books for studying the life of David are *The Life of David as Reflected in His Psalms* by Alexander Maclaren (London: Hodder & Stoughton, 1888), and *A Harmony of Samuel, Kings and Chronicles* by William Day Crockett (Grand Rapids: Baker, 1964).

WWW

The man after God's own heart (1 Sam. 13:14; Ps. 89:20; Acts 13:22). Note the "key of David" (Isa. 22:15–25; Rev. 3:7), the "root of David" (Rev. 5:5), and the "root and offspring of David" (Rev. 22:16). David was known for the skill of his hands and the integrity of his heart (Ps. 78:70–72). God's gentleness made him great (Ps. 18:35).

WWW

David's life illustrates the old adage, "Life is 10 percent what you make it and 90 percent how you take it." Of course, David could "take it" because he trusted the Lord and obeyed Him.

WWW

One of the purposes of the book of Ruth is to explain how David came on the scene. He was related to a Moabitess (see Deut. 23:3), yet God graciously accepted Ruth (Ruth 2:21) and therefore accepted David. See Ruth 4:13–22.

WWW

God sought a man (1 Sam. 13:14), found him (Ps. 89:20), chose him (Ps. 78:70), and appointed him (1 Sam. 13:14), and thereby provided a king (1 Sam. 16:1).

WWW

Few have had so varied a career as he: shepherd and monarch; poet and soldier; champion of his people, and an outlaw in the caves of Judea; beloved of Jonathan and persecuted by Saul; vanquishing the Philistines one day, and accompanying them into battle on another . . .

F. B. Meyer, *David: Shepherd, Psalmist, King*, p. 17

It may be that Abraham excelled him in faith, and Moses in the power of concentrated fellowship with God, and Elijah in the fiery force of enthusiasm. But none of these was so many-sided as the richly-gifted son of Jesse.

Meyer, *David,* p. 17

Sometimes we have to march, sometimes to halt; now we are called to action, again to suffering; in the battle to rush forward like a torrent, in the next to glide stealthily to ambush and wait. We must admit nothing stereotyped in our methods.

Meyer, *David,* p. 155

A throne is God's purpose for you; a cross is God's path for you; faith is God's plan for you.

Alan Redpath, *The Making of a Man of God,* p. 65

Goliath (1 Samuel 17)

I am sure that the top-brass Israelites spent every day discussing ways and means to deal with the giant and defeat the Philistines. Then, one day, little David came along and it was all over. . . . The answer was not in growing a Goliath but in developing a David, and that is exactly what God was doing in the solitudes around Bethlehem.

Vance Havner, *Why Not Just Be Christians?* p. 67

It was there that the victory over Goliath was really won. To have lost his temper in this unproductive assault would have broken the alliance of his soul with God, and drawn a veil over the sense of His presence. [On David's self-control when his brother criticized him. See 1 Sam. 17:28–29.]

Meyer, *David,* p. 43

King Saul

But the moment the world discovers what you are, when the obvious evidence of heavenly reality rests upon you, they will begin to sling the javelins at you. Also, as in the case of David, you will discover that the place of rejection by others is the place of acceptance by God.

Redpath, *Making of a Man,* p. 18

This illustrates the fact that it often requires as much godly resolution to restrain the excesses of zealous but unspiritual friends as it does to stand firm against the rage of incensed enemies. [On the two occasions when David had the opportunity to kill King Saul and refused, even though some of his best men advised him to do it. See 1 Samuel 24, 26.]

Arthur W. Pink, *The Life of David,* 1:163

Nabal (1 Samuel 25)

David was patient with King Saul who tried to kill him, but he lost his temper over Nabal's unkindness and would have murdered him were it not for Abigail. See Proverbs 15:1 and 25:11–12, and Psalm 141:5.

WWW

Three approaches to life are illustrated in the Nabal event: like Nabal, we can return evil for good; like David, we can return evil for evil; or like Abigail, we can return good for evil. See Romans 12:17–21.

WWW

However long I may have been on the Christian path, however often I may have overcome one temptation or another, however many times I have defeated sin in one area it can strike in another and crush me in a moment.

Redpath, *Making of a Man,* p. 107

The Cup of Cold Water (2 Sam. 23:13–17; 1 Chron. 11:15–19)

How often we sigh for the waters of the well of Bethlehem! We go back on our past and dwell on never-to-be-forgotten memories.

Meyer, *David,* p. 164

Great services reveal our possibilities; small services reveal our consecration.

GHM, Return of the Angels, p. 113

When asked to write his memoirs of the Civil War, General Robert E. Lee refused and explained, "I should be trading on the blood of my men."

Henry II, King of England from 1133 to 1189, had a running battle with the church, especially with Thomas à Becket, archbishop of Canterbury. One day the king lamented, "What sluggish knaves I have brought up in my kingdom! Is there no one who will rid me of this turbulent priest?" Four of his gentlemen caught the message and rode to Canterbury, where they found the archbishop and killed him. Neither David nor Henry actually issued orders, but their men received the king's desires as their commands. O that God's people today would be that close to the Lord to discover the desires of His heart and fulfill them!

WWW

Bringing Up the Ark (2 Samuel 6)

Just as David borrowed his idea from the Philistines, the church today has borrowed from the world the vehicles of her ministry. We study the techniques of this age, the gadgetry of the business, social, and entertainment world, looking for new carts on which to carry the ark of our testimony. We hold a wet finger in the air to ascertain which way the popular wind is blowing; we set our sails to catch the latest breeze. Instead of asking, "How does God do it?" we ask, "How does the world do it?" We are religious copy-cats.

Vance Havner, Moments of Decision, pp. 46–47

The biggest business before the church today is to get the work of God off the new carts, and back on the shoulders of separated men and women. Too many Philistines run the church today. . . . God's work must be done by God's people in God's way.

Havner, Moments of Decision, p. 51

Deep Disappointment (2 Samuel 7)

During his many wars, David regularly took a portion of the spoils to be placed in the treasury of the Lord. His plan was to use the treasure for building the temple, but God told him he was not to build it. This was a great disappointment in David's life.

WWW

Some day we shall understand that God has a reason in every "no" which He speaks through the slow movement of life. He would reveal it to us if we could bear it; but it is better not to pry into the mystery of His providence.

Meyer, *David*, p. 183

David committed adultery with Bathsheba and married her, and from this union Solomon was born (2 Sam. 12:24–25). David became proud and numbered the people, and because of this sin, seventy thousand people died (2 Samuel 24). To stop the plague, David purchased a piece of property, erected an altar, and offered sacrifices to the Lord. One day, Solomon built the temple on that very piece of property! David didn't build the temple, but out of David's two worst sins God built a temple to His glory (see Rom. 5:20).

WWW

Bathsheba (2 Samuel 11–12)

The Bible never flatters its heroes. It tells us the truth about each one of them in order that against the background of human breakdown and failure we may magnify the grace of God and recognize that it is the delight of the Spirit of God to work upon the platform of human impossibilities.

Redpath, *Making of a Man*, p. 5

But the most deadly evils do not *leap* on us. The most deadly evils *creep* on us. And it is that slow and silent growth of all that at last is mighty to confound, which lulls men into the strange security which always is the associate of self-ignorance.

GHM, *The Afterglow of God,* p. 382

A great man cannot commit a small sin.

Alfonso "the Wise," King of Castile and Leon (1252–84)

Let us beware of our light, unguarded hours. Moments of leisure are more to be dreaded than those at strenuous toil. Middle life—for David was above fifty years of age—has no immunity from temptations and perils which beset the young.

Meyer, *David,* p. 195

The better the man, the dearer he pays for a short season of sinful pleasure.

Meyer, *David,* p. 196

The wonder of all righteousness is this, that its tomorrow is brighter than yesterday. The certainty of sin is always this, that its tomorrow is a little worse.

GHM, *Return of the Angels,* p. 221

Sin is dark, dangerous, damnable; but it cannot stanch the love of God, it cannot change the love that is not of yesterday, but dates from eternity itself.

Meyer, *David,* p. 199

The good things in life we pay for in advance; the bad things, on the installment plan.

David, a "Salvation Army Cadet"

General William Booth, founder of the Salvation Army, used to preach a sermon to new recruits in which he compared David to a Salvation Army cadet. David was a volunteer, "unskilled and undrilled" in the rules of war, but he became a successful soldier and leader. He was despised, chaffed, and sneered at, yet he did

his job and honored the Lord. He had confidence in himself and
in his Lord. He is an example of what the "Christian soldier" ought
to be (2 Tim. 2:1–4).

Deborah

She is the only woman in the Bible who is placed at the height
of political power by the common consent of her people. Other
females have reigned besides Deborah—but not by the suffrages
of the people. Jezebel reigned, Athaliah reigned; but their empire
was regarded with hatred by the community. . . . But Deborah had
no royal lineage. She was the wife of an obscure man. She was the
head of a humble household unknown to the people of Israel.

GM-RWB, 151

Demas

Three texts tell the whole story, and a sad one it is. "Demas . . .
[one of] my fellow laborers" (Philem. 24); "Demas" (Col. 4:14);
and "Demas has forsaken me, having loved this present world
[age]" (2 Tim. 4:10). Jesus has delivered us from "the present
evil age" (Gal. 1:4), and yet it exerts a strong pull and captures
many professed believers. First there is friendship with the world
(James 4:4), then we are spotted by the world (James 1:27), then
we love the world (1 John 2:15–17) and start conforming to the
world (Rom. 12:2). The result? We are condemned with the world
(1 Cor. 11:32), as was Lot, who lost everything (Gen. 19).

WWW

He was not a monster, but just a man like the rest of us; and he
came to his bad eminence by a well-trodden and familiar path.

Alexander Maclaren, *Expositions of Scripture* (2 Tim. 4:10–11)

Then I saw in my dream, that a little off the road, over against the
silver mine, stood Demas (gentleman-like) to call to passengers

[travelers] to come and see; who said to Christian and his fellow, Ho! Turn aside hither, and I will show you a thing.

CHRISTIAN: What thing so deserving as to turn us out of the way to see it?

DEMAS: Here is a silver mine, and some digging in it for treasure. If you will come, with a little pains you may richly provide for yourselves.

Then said Hopeful, Let us go see.

CHRISTIAN: Not I, said Christian, I have heard of this place before now; and how many have there been slain; and besides that, treasure is a snare to those who seek it; for it hindereth them in their pilgrimage. . . .

Then Christian roundly answered, saying, Demas, thou art an enemy to the right ways of the Lord of this way, and hast already been condemned for thine own turning aside by one of His Majesty's judges (2 Tim. 4:10). . . .

DEMAS: Yes, my name is Demas; I am the son of Abraham.

CHRISTIAN: I know you; Gehazi was your great-grandfather, and Judas your father; and you have trod in their steps [2 Kings 5:20; Matt. 26:14–15; 27:1–5]. It is but a devilish prank that thou usest; thy father was hanged for a traitor, and thou deservest no better reward. . . . Thus they went their way.

John Bunyan, *The Pilgrim's Progress*

Some preachers are forsaking Paul today, forsaking what he stood for and the standard he raised: the Pauline theology, manner of life, and view of the future. They tell us that Jesus came simply to teach a Gospel of love, but Paul built a complicated system of doctrine, including ecclesiology, ethics and eschatology that are out of date today. His views on the inspiration of the Scriptures, sin, blood atonement, salvation, separation from the world, Christian conduct and the future do not fit the image of clergymen who wear mod attire, use Madison Avenue techniques, hobnob with Sodom and Gomorrah, chatter gaily in the new language of the avant-garde, and are more like the happiness boys on television than holy men of God.

Havner, *Moments of Decision,* p. 119

Doeg (1 Samuel 21–22; Psalm 52)

When we come to this man Doeg, we feel like leaving out the "e" and letting it stand as just plain "dog."

CEM, *Chariots of Fire*, p. 82

Doeg was a past master of the art of defamation of character by slander. . . . Everything that Doeg reported was true . . . but it was told in such a way and told at such a time, as to leave the impression in the mind of Saul that Ahimelech was in conspiracy against him.

CEM, *Chariots of Fire*, pp. 84–85

The slanderer is the submarine of human society, prowling submerged in darkness and discharging his missile at those who go up and down the paths of life on errands of peace and good will.

CEM, *Chariots of Fire*, p. 85

E

Ehud (Judg. 3:12–30)

In Latin, the word meaning "left-handed" is *sinister*. In English, the word *sinister* means "dangerous, suspicious, evil, ominous." Why? Because a soldier who was left-handed could distract an opponent with his right hand and then stab him with the left.

WWW

Unusual weapons during the days of the Judges: an ox goad (Judg. 3:31); a tent peg (Judg. 4:22); pitchers or jars (Judg. 7:20); a millstone (Judg. 9:53); a jawbone (Judg. 15:15). See also 1 Corinthians 1:26–29.

Eleazar (2 Sam. 23:9–10)

Happy are they who can follow a good cause in its worst estate, for theirs is true glory.

CHS, 56:181

This man Eleazar, however, made up for the failures of his countrymen, for "he arose and smote the Philistines." He was a man of marked individuality of character, a man who knew himself and knew his God, and did not care to be lost in the common mass, so as to run away merely because they ran. He thought for himself, and acted for himself; he did not make the conduct of others the measure of his service; but while Israel fled, "he arose and smote the Philistines.". . . I do not find that he wasted time in upbraiding the others for running away, nor in shouting to them to return; but he just turned his own face to the enemy, and hewed and hacked away with all his might.

CHS, 56:182

When we have a good work to do for our Lord, we are glad of the company of kindred spirits, determined to make the good work succeed; but if we have no such comrades, we must go alone.

CHS, 56:183

"The people returned after him only to spoil" (v. 10). Eleazar was pleased to see them in the field again. I daresay he did not say one rebuking word to them, but perhaps remarked, "Well, you have come back, have you? Share the plunder among yourselves. I might claim it all myself, but I will not; you are welcome to it."

CHS, 56:188

How many courageous leaders have fought the battles and others have claimed the spoils! It isn't important who gets the credit or the spoils, but that God gets the glory.

WWW

Eli

The first point remarkable in him is the absence of envy. Eli furthers Samuel's advancement, and assists it to his own detriment.

F. W. Robertson, *Sermons,* 4:4

Eli's feelings were all good; his acts were all wrong. In sentiment Eli might always be trusted; in action he was forever false, because he was a weak, vacillating man.

F. W. Robertson, *Sermons,* 4:11

Elijah

He suddenly appears as the crisis-prophet, with thunder on his brow and tempest in his voice. He disappears just as suddenly, being swept away in a chariot of fire.

J. Sidlow Baxter, Mark These Men, p. 11

Elijah was a praying fighter. He won his greatest battles upon his knees. (James 5:17)

Clovis Chappell, And the Prophets, p. 51

He had a consuming passion for the glory of God. He was content to be a slave of Jehovah. He was implicitly obedient to the divine commands.

J. Oswald Sanders, On to Maturity, p. 174

We need such anger today. It is fine to be tolerant. To fail to be so is to fail to be Christian. But much of our so-called tolerance is not tolerance at all but indifference. . . . There is no surer sign that one's moral nature has become flabby and honeycombed than a lost capacity for unselfish anger.

Chappell, And the Prophets, pp. 49–50

The man who enters a place of public service . . . must be *alone with God*; his spirit must be exercised in private; he must pass through the deep waters in his own experience, otherwise he will be but a theorist, and not a witness; his ear must be opened to hear, ere his tongue can be fitted to speak as the learned.

C. H. Mackintosh, Life and Times of Elijah, p. 11

We must be kept low. . . . Our time of *training in secret* must far exceed our time of *acting in public*.

Mackintosh, Elijah, p. 21

The man of faith must be emptied from vessel to vessel; each successive scene and stage of the believer's life is but his entrance upon a new form [level] in the school of Christ, where he has to learn some fresh and, of course, more difficult lessons.

Mackintosh, Elijah, p. 36

Because of our proneness to look at the bucket and forget the fountain, God has frequently to change His means of supply to keep our eyes fixed on Him.

Watchman Nee

Though the stream must fail, the fountain is still full and still flowing.

John Newton

1 Kings 18

In our day, the greatest lack in the life of the individual Christian and of the Church is the fire of God, the manifested presence and mighty working of the Holy Spirit. . . . Our lives are not fire-touched.

Sanders, *On to Maturity,* p. 177

The immortal test of Elijah, made in the presence of an apostate king, and in the face of a backslidden nation and an idolatrous priesthood on Mount Carmel, is a sublime exhibition of faith and prayer.

E. M. Bounds

I am sure, if God hadn't held him back, Satan would have brought up a little spark out of hell to set that sacrifice on fire. But God wouldn't let him.

Moody, *Words, Work, and Workers,* p. 157

1 Kings 19

Elijah was a great man, but he was still only a man "of like nature" as we are. He was not the first servant of God to get discouraged in the work and want to quit or die. Consider Moses (Num. 11:15), Jonah (Jonah 4:3), David (Ps. 55:6), Jeremiah (Jer. 9:1–2), and even Paul (2 Cor. 1:8–11). "The best of men are but men at their best."

WWW

Elijah's experiences on Mount Carmel and afterward illustrate Isaiah 40:31. At the altar, he mounted up with wings as the eagle and defeated the pagan priests. He ran before Ahab's chariot and did not get weary, and he walked in the wilderness to Mount Horeb and did not faint (1 Kings 19:1–8). But in running away from the place of duty, the prophet disobeyed the Lord and walked by sight and not by faith.

WWW

"I only am left." See Psalm 12:1; Isaiah 57:1; 63:5; Jeremiah 5:1; 15:1–4; and Micah 7:2.

Nothing but abiding faith in the Word of God can maintain anyone in the path of service, because *faith makes a man satisfied to wait for the end,* whereas unbelief, looking only at surrounding circumstances, sinks into complete despondency.

Mackintosh, *Elijah,* p. 93

When you get in the dumps and fret and fume and wish you were dead, just stop right there and tell yourself that you are a liar. . . . A lot of blue people need rest from idleness. One big reason why they are blue is because they have nothing else to do.

Clovis Chappell, *Sermons on Biblical Characters,* p. 125

Now, what the Lord wanted Elijah to learn is just what He wants you and me to learn, that our job in this world is not bookkeeping.

Chappell, *Sermons on Biblical Characters,* 126

He thought there was not a good man in Israel. And if you want a short cut to wretchedness, get to a place where you do not believe in anybody.

Chappell, *Sermons on Biblical Characters,* p. 122

But Elijah, if you die, there will be an end of the Lord's people, if your reckoning is correct. Surely, if you are the only one left, you ought to pray that you may live on until there are some more to carry on the work. . . . He prayed that he might die; why? Because he was afraid that he should die! That is the odd thing about his request: he was running away from Jezebel, because she had threatened to kill him, yet he prayed that he might die.

CHS, 47:210–11

At Mount Carmel, Elijah walked by faith and vindicated the Lord. But at Mount Horeb, he walked in unbelief and tried to vindicate himself and also accuse the whole nation.

For He knows our frame; He remembers that we are dust.

Psalm 103:14 NKJV

2 Kings 2

Bethel had ceased to be the house of God save in name; Gilgal was no longer valued as the place where the reproach of Egypt had been rolled away. The walls of Jericho which had been destroyed by faith, were built again. Jordan was no longer viewed as the scene of Jehovah's power. In a word, all these things had become form without power. [See Amos 5:4–6.]

Mackintosh, *Elijah,* p. 111

The Transfiguration (Matt. 17:1–13)

He [Jesus] had reached a crisis in the process of the work, and they [Moses and Elijah] came to greet Him in the moment of triumph, and to speak with Him of the work yet remaining to be done. By their conversation with Him they revealed the interest of the dwellers in heaven in His approaching work, for they talked with Him of the exodus which He was about to accomplish.

GCM, *The Crises of the Christ,* p. 235

Elisha

Elisha is a different personality. Elisha is not the copyist. Elisha is not the echo. Elisha stands out in his own unspoiled individuality.

George W. Truett, *The Prophet's Mantle,* p. 17

Work out your own salvation with fear and trembling.

Philippians 2:12

Elijah had taught his friend that no man is indispensable. Therefore Elisha asked not, "Where is Elijah?" but "Where is the Lord
God of Elijah?" The need of our day is not this prophet or that
prophet, this man or that man. The big need of our day, and of
every day, is God.

Chappell, *And the Prophets*, p. 52

We know where the Lord God of Elijah is—on the throne of
heaven. *But where are the Elijahs?*

Enoch

He preached the Second Coming (Jude 14–15), practiced the Second
Coming (Heb. 11:5–6; 1 John 3:1–3), and pictured the Second
Coming (Gen. 5:21–24; 1 Thess. 4:13–18).

WWW

Enoch's Day (Gen. 4:17–24; 6:1–8)

They became famous and skilful in all the works of this life: one
was called the father of shepherds, and another the father of mu-
sicians; but we read of none that was a father of faithful lambs in
Christ's flock, of none that was the father of children who made
God's statutes their song in the house of their pilgrimage. (See
Ps. 119:54.)

Ryle, *The True Christian*, p. 233

To walk with God is to be always going forward, always pressing
on, never standing still and flattering ourselves that we are the men
and have borne much fruit; but to grow in grace, to go on from
strength to strength, to forget the things behind, and if by grace
we have attained unto anything, to abound yet more and more.

Ryle, *The True Christian*, p. 238

If it be a marvelous thing that Enoch walked with God, it is a more marvelous thing that God walked with Enoch, waiting for him as for a weak child along the way.

GCM, 5:68–69

When he changes mere "living" into "walking with God," he goes over precisely the same ground—he is still occupied with the care of "sons and daughters." No outward eye could have detected the difference. Religion is not a change of space; it is a change of spirit. It is not a new road, but a new perception. It finds its earliest glory in retracing the old way. Enoch, in his vegetating days, has gone the round of certain household duties, has borne certain burdens which as a parent he was bound to bear. When he begins to walk with God he walks on the same path where he had vegetated. He repeats the old duties with a new light in his soul. He bears the old burdens with a new strength in his arm. He meets the old faces with a new love in his heart. He treads again the path which he trod yesterday; but yesterday he walked alone, today he walks with God.

GM-RMB, 1:76–77

Esau

He is called a "profane person" (Heb. 12:16 KJV). Modern translations use words such as "godless," "irreverent," "irreligious," and "careless about God." The English word *profane* comes from the Latin *profanus* and means "outside the temple, common, ordinary, not sacred." His mind and heart were accessible to everybody; he had no boundaries or walls that set him apart for God. The Vulgate uses this Latin word for "what may be used freely." Because Esau did not know God, he was open to everybody and everything.

WWW

He was a profane person, not in the sense of taking God's name in vain—there is no suggestion of that—but in the sense of never feeling and recognizing God's claim upon him at all.

Strahan, *Hebrew Ideals*, p. 207

In every incident [in Esau's life] we find a new reason, a new passion, a new motive; a profane person, a temple with the doors open, and all the unhallowed crowds tramping in and out, walking across the threshold, no sanctity, no sacredness, no reserve, no consciousness of high and holy things, no recognition of principle, no sense of responsibility.

GCM, *26 Sermons*, 3:102

He sold his birthright for a mess of pottage, and he thought he would buy it back by giving his father a mess of pottage. . . . This is what sinners say. "I have lost heaven by my evil works; I will easily get it back by reforming."

CHS, 5:119

There was no reason for Esau to exaggerate his situation and say he was at the point of death. His father Isaac was a very wealthy man and there was plenty of food in the camp. Why did he sell his birthright? *Because he despised it and had no interest in spiritual things—and everybody knew it!* (See Gen. 25:34 and Heb. 12:16.)

WWW

Esau voluntarily gave up his own birthright. And the doctrine is, that every man who loses heaven gives it up himself. Every man who loses everlasting life rejects it himself. God denies it not to him—he will not come that he may have life.

CHS, 5:118

But though the past is irrevocable, it is not irreparable. . . . God Himself cannot undo the past, but He can and will forgive. He will not mention the past, but give us a fair fresh start.

F. B. Meyer, *Israel: A Prince with God,* p. 31

There are no trifles in Christian living. Everything is great; because the mightiest events revolve on the smallest pivots; and the greatest harvests for good and ill spring from the tiniest seeds.

Meyer, *Israel*, pp. 27–28

Genesis 33

While Jacob remembered the dark threat (Gen. 27:41), Esau himself forgot it. His sudden blaze of anger, instead of smoldering down to a life-long hatred, quite died out; and on Jacob's return to Canaan, "Esau ran to meet him. . . ." Esau might be reckless and impulsive, but he was not malevolent; he was quicker to forgive than to blame; and when his heart was touched, the strong man wept like a woman.

Strahan, *Hebrew Ideals,* p. 259

Esther

The Lord's wisdom is seen in arranging the smallest events so as to produce great results.

CHS, 20:619

Remember, for your humiliation, that *God can do without you.* . . . When He looked and there was no man, His own arm brought Him salvation. [Esther 4:13–17; Isa. 63:5]

CHS, 20:233

Ezekiel

The word *sword* is used 82 times in the Hebrew text of Ezekiel's prophecy.

Like Jeremiah and John the Baptist, Ezekiel was born to be a priest but was called to be a prophet, a much more difficult ministry. The Law of Moses instructed the priest in his duties, but the prophet had to receive fresh messages day after day to know what the Lord wanted him to do. A priest ministered to keep the people walking with God, but the prophet was sent by God to bring the people back to His way. A priest was rarely in danger, but a prophet was often looked upon as the enemy of the people, especially of the apostate establishment.

WWW

Ezekiel records the departure of the glory of God from the temple in Jerusalem: 8:1–4; 9:1–3; 10:1–4, 18; 11:22–23. He also promises that the glory will return (43:1–5).

F

Felix (Acts 24)

The name Felix means "happy" but history reveals him as a man who "indulged in every kind of barbarity and lust" and "exercised the power of a king in the spirit of a slave" (Tacitus, *The Histories*, 5.9). His wife Drusilla, daughter of Herod Agrippa, was as wicked as her husband.

What the apostle did, every minister ought to do. He selected a topic appropriate to the occasion.

CHS, 4:51

[Paul] preached Jesus Christ at the very moment he was persecuted for having preached Him. He preached even when in chains. He did more; he attacked his judge on the throne. He reasoned, he enforced, he thundered.

Jacques Saurin, "Paul Before Felix and Drusilla," in Treasury of the World's Great Sermons, ed. Warren W. Wiersbe, p. 505

Paul struck the chord of righteousness and justice which underlie the universe. Righteousness and judgment are the habitation [foundation] of God's throne [Ps. 89:14; 97:2].

CEM, Bible Epitaphs, p. 144

There are those who can preach to the crowd. It takes a man with a vision of the Cross to preach to two people. . . .

Gipsy Smith, *As Jesus Passed By,* p. 137

What a surprising scene, my brethren, is here presented to your view. The governor trembled, and the captive spoke without dismay. The captive made the governor tremble. The governor shuddered in the presence of the captive.

Saurin, p. 506

O marvelous power of a preached gospel! O mighty truth that God is with the ministry, when the kings of the earth that take counsel together are yet dismayed by it! Who is he that does not see here something more than human eloquence, when a prisoner becomes the judge and the prince upon the throne becomes the criminal?

CHS, 4:52

The purpose of preaching is not to make people comfortable, to cast them into a moral stupor, to fill their mind with illusion, but to awaken their conscience.

CEM, *Bible Epitaphs,* p. 147

Thank God for pain! It keeps off death many a time. And in like manner thank God for a swift conscience that speaks. It is meant to ring an alarm-bell to us and make us, as the Bible has it, "flee for refuge to the hope that is before us."

Alexander Maclaren, *A Year's Ministry,* p. 168

His thought is to get rid of Paul and his disturbing message for the present. But he does not wish to shut the door altogether. He gives a sop to his conscience to stop its barking, and he probably deceives himself as to the gravity of his present decision by the lightly-given and well-guarded promise with its indefiniteness, "When I have a more convenient season, I will send for thee."

Maclaren, *A Year's Ministry,* p. 167

Felix trembled, but he did not repent. Felix was a victim of tomorrow. If today has slain its thousands, tomorrow has slain its tens of thousands.

CEM, *Bible Epitaphs,* p. 141

All the great opportunities of life are opportunities of today and not of tomorrow.

CEM, *Bible Epitaphs,* p. 149

The road of bye-and-bye leads to the house of never.

Spanish Proverb

G

Gamaliel (Acts 5:33–42)

Gamaliel had been set in his high seat by the God of Israel in order that he might watch for the coming Messiah and might announce His advent to the people of Israel.

AW-BC, p. 568

And we all make Gamaliel's tremendous and irreparable mistake when we approach Jesus Christ and His cause and His Kingdom on the side of policy, and when we handle Him as a matter open to argument and debate. He is not a matter of argument and debate; He is an ambassador of reconciliation. We are simply not permitted to sit in judgment on Almighty God and on His message of mercy to us.

AW-BC, p. 568

He was held in repute by the people; but the people were blind, and they loved to be led by blind leaders. And Gamaliel was one of them.

AW-BC, p. 569

Gideon

If we only cry, "The sword of the Lord!" we shall be guilty of an idle presumption. . . . This is the cry of every lie-a-bed. . . . Nor must it be "The sword of Gideon" alone, for that were idolatrous reliance on an arm of the flesh. We can do nothing of ourselves.

CHS, 10:167

How difficult it was for [Gideon] to fight the enemy at these odds. If I had been there, I'd have befouled my breeches for fright.

Martin Luther

I see, and you must see, men every day who are as brave and as bold as Gideon, and as full of anger and revenge against all the wrongs and all the miseries of their fellow-men; men and women who take their lives in their hands to do battle with ignorance and vice and all the other evils that the land lies under; and, all the time, they go on repeating Gideon's fatal mistake; till, at the end of their lives, they leave all these wrongs and miseries very much as they found them: nothing better, but rather worse. And all because they set up an ephod of their own devising in the place of the ephod and the altar and the sacrifice and the intercession that God has set up for those and all other evils.

AW-BC, p. 87

H

Habakkuk

Men of faith are always the men that have to confront problems. Blot God out, and your problems are all ended. If there is no God in heaven, then we have no problem about sin and suffering. . . . But the moment you admit the existence of an all-powerful governing God, you are face to face with your problems. If you say that you have none, I question the strength of your faith.

GCM, *The Minor Prophets*, p. 99

[Habakkuk 2:4] Today there are two principles of life in the world and only two. The principle of the "puffed up," who are self-centered and conditioned by circumstance; and the principle of the righteous by faith, who are God-centered and God-circumferenced.

GCM, *The Minor Prophets*, p. 100

Hagar

God did not urge Hagar stubbornly to nurse her grief and keep alive her hate. He did not tell her to live for the one purpose of getting even with the man who had wronged her. The roadway of anger and of bitter resentment never leads out of the desert. . . .

Nursing your wrongs and your burning hate is never a path to an oasis. Hagar must leave God to deal with Abraham, as you must leave God to deal with the one who has wronged you.

Clovis Chappell, *Sermons on Old Testament Characters,* p. 57

Hannah (1 Samuel 1–2)

She was one of the barren women in Scripture whom the Lord graciously enabled to become mothers: Sarah (Gen. 18:1–15); Rebekah (Gen. 25:19–26); Rachel (Gen. 30:22–24; 35:16–20); and Elizabeth (Luke 1:5–25).

Hannah "poured out her soul" to the Lord (1 Sam. 1:15). See Job 3:24; Psalms 42:4; 62:8; 102:1; 142:2; Lamentations 2:11, 19.

Hannah's husband must have ratified the vow she made to the Lord (Num. 30:6–15), for he had the power to nullify it. They were in agreement (1 Peter 3:7). They wanted a son who would serve God and lead the nation back to the Lord.

WWW

The story of Hannah introduces a new name for the Lord, "the Lord of hosts," used nearly three hundred times in the Old Testament (1 Sam. 1:3, 11). Jehovah is the Lord of the armies in heaven and on earth. (The NIV translates "Lord Sabaoth" as "Lord Almighty.") See 2 Samuel 5:10; 6:2, 18; 7:8, 26–27; Psalms 24:10; 46:7, 11; 48:8; Isaiah 1:9; Romans 9:29; James 5:4.

WWW

1 Samuel 2:18–21

Mothers still make garments for their children . . . by their holy and enabling characters displayed from day to day before young and quickly-observant eyes, by their words and conversation, and by the habits of daily devotion.

F. B. Meyer, *Samuel the Prophet,* p. 22

Herod

The Herod clan was Edomite in ancestry, descendants of Esau; so what they did to the Jews and Christians was only a continuation of the conflict between Esau and Jacob, the flesh versus the Spirit. They were murderers. Herod the Great tried to kill the child Jesus by slaying the innocent children in Bethlehem (Matthew 2). During his reign he also killed three of his own sons, a son-in-law, and a favorite wife. Herod Antipas, son of Herod the Great, killed John the Baptist, and Herod the Great's grandson Herod Agrippa killed the apostle James (Acts 12).

WWW

Herod Antipas (Mark 6:14–29; Luke 23:6–12)

Antipas was a weak, cruel, sensual, ostentatious, shallow-hearted creature. . . . His licentious life, his family miseries, his political maneuvers, his sycophantic and extravagant expenditures, his ruinous defeats, both in war and in diplomacy, his fall from his throne, and his banishment from his kingdom, all are to be read in the books of Josephus.

AW-BC, p. 525

Herod was, after a sort, a follower of John, but never a follower of Jesus. It is easy for you to hear the preacher and love and admire him, and yet the preacher's Master may be all unknown to you. The goal of all our ministry is Christ Jesus.

CHS, 26:404

Herod had already silenced the voice. . . . For what was John? He said, "I am the voice of one crying in the wilderness." What was Jesus but the Word? He that silences the voice may well be denied the Word.

CHS, 28:103

Herod's day of grace had lasted long, but now it is at an end. Herod had many opportunities, and at one time he was almost

84

persuaded. . . . Herod had smothered and silenced his conscience long ago and now he is to be forever left alone.

AW-BC, p. 526

Hezekiah (2 Kings 20:12–13; Isaiah 39)

Here is a prosperous man, in a proud state of heart, with grace at a low ebb in his spirit; he is now ready to be the prey of temptation.

CHS, 12:438

He does not appear to have said a word to them about Jehovah. Would it have been polite? Etiquette, now a days, often demands of a Christian that he should not intrude his religion upon company. Out on such etiquette! It is the etiquette of hell!

CHS, 12:440

"Hezekiah was glad of them" (2 Kings 20:12–13). . . . He was very pleased to see them. It is an ill sign when a Christian takes great solace in the company of the worldling, more especially when that worldling is profane. . . . Courtesy is due from the Christian to all men, but the unholy intimacy which allows a believer to receive an unregenerate as his bosom friend is sin.

CHS, 12:139

I

Isaac

So far as fame is concerned, Isaac had the misfortune to come between two of the greatest and most striking personalities of the Bible, Abraham, who was his father, and Jacob, who was his son. Isaac was not an innovator. There is nothing striking or dramatic or thrilling in his life, with the exception of his father Abraham offering him up on Mount Moriah. . . . Yet Isaac carried on the great tradition of faith in God, and was a necessary link in the chain of the divine purpose and destiny. Some men are great in what they initiate and discover; others are great in what they preserve or rediscover. The last was preeminently true of Isaac.

CEM, *The Wisest Fool and Other Men of the Bible*, p. 21

Isaac's chief characteristic is a fine sensibility. He is keenly alive both to the joys and the sorrows of life.

Strahan, *Hebrew Ideals*, p. 194

Abraham is more interesting than Isaac, and Jacob is more interesting than Isaac, to us, but not to God.

GCM, *26 Sermons*, 3:78–79

At Gerar (Genesis 26)

Abraham would have reproved Abimelech (Gen. 21:25). . . . Jacob would have outwitted them. . . . Isaac won by non-resistance, by quiet persistence, quiet patience.

GCM, *26 Sermons,* 3:83

Isaiah (chapter 6)

The young prophet was a hero worshipper and King Uzziah was his hero. . . . The young prophet was shocked by the king's death but he was challenged and his faith was strengthened by the vision he had in the temple. He was pointed to the truth that God is the true source of the people's help.

Truett, *The Prophet's Mantle,* pp. 171–72

He found that God in His providence includes and utilizes the dark days and hours of the experiences of life, just as He does the bright sunshine.

Truett, *The Prophet's Mantle,* p. 176

He saw the people as he had never seen them before. He was a fortunate young man, according to worldly standards. He moved in the upper strata of society. He was at home in the king's palace. He was in that group which had prestige and prominence and power. But when his beloved king died, he "saw the Lord high and lifted up." Then his whole view of life was changed. Then he saw the people in their downtrodden state. . . . He saw human needs. He saw human responsibility. He saw human anguish and suffering as he had never seen them before.

Truett, *The Prophet's Mantle,* p. 178

The prophet's call in Isaiah 6 preceded what he wrote in the first five chapters of the book. Isaiah said "Woe is me!" (6:5) before he pronounced the six woes upon the sinners in the land as recorded in Isaiah 5.

WWW

Behind the empty throne, there is a throne that is never empty. Over the chaos that appalls the heart there is a God of order and government.

GCM, 2:298

The Lord is always upon a throne; even when He is nailed to the Cross, this Lord and His throne are inseparable.

Joseph Parker, *The People's Bible,* 14:283

It is the throne of absolute sovereignty; of resistless, questionless supremacy over all. The Lord reigneth; Thy throne, O God, is for ever and ever.

R. S. Candlish, *Sermons,* p. 88

It is a signal instance of grace on the part of the Lord that I am allowed to be a volunteer. . . . His servant is not coerced or constrained, as with bit and bridle. He has the unspeakable privilege and happiness of giving himself voluntarily . . . to the Lord, who willingly gave Himself for him.

Candlish, *Sermons,* p. 98

But the most stupendous evidence of God's grace is that when He saves me He consents to use me. And, my brethren, one of the first qualifications for being ready is to have stood in the presence of His glory, and to have found out how unworthy I am to utter His message. . . . Every day I am more astonished that God should use me at all.

GCM, 2:303

Men are never duly troubled and impressed with a conviction of their insignificance until they have contrasted themselves with the majesty of God.

John Calvin

J

Jacob

Evaluations of Jacob and his character go from one extreme to the other. Some see him as a misjudged man who was not a schemer but the victim of the schemes of others. See *I Have Loved Jacob* by Joseph Hoffman Cohn (Orangeburg, NY: American Board of Missions to the Jews, 1948). Others do not see one good thing in him at all. Whatever we may think about Jacob, let's remember that God loved him (Mal. 1:2; Rom. 9:13) and deigned to be called "the God of Jacob," and that Jacob was the father of the twelve tribes of Israel.

There is no record that the Lord personally condemned Jacob for what he did and said, although he did chasten Jacob and allow his sins to find him out. Jacob's life is certainly shrouded in conflict—with Esau in the womb (Gen. 25:22) and afterward, with his wives, with Laban, and with the Lord; but the Lord never deserted him (Gen. 28:15). Some students see in Abraham the image of the Father who gives his Son, in Isaac the Son who gives his life, and in Jacob the conflict between the flesh and the Spirit. The period from Jacob's birth to his flight from home covers seventy-five years. From Bethel to Peniel is a period of twenty years. From Peniel to his death, fifty-two years. W. Graham Scroggie saw in the first period Jacob the natural man, in the second period Jacob the carnal man, and in the third period Jacob the spiritual man

(*A Treasury of W. Graham Scroggie,* ed. Ralph G. Turnbull [Grand Rapids: Baker, 1974], 139–43).

WWW

How like our own is Jacob's history! Until God begins to deal with us, we are inclined to take a superior attitude to Jacob's intrigues, but as we begin to encounter the deviousness of our own thinking, we soon recognize the man's essential character in ourselves. And remember, what changed Jacob's life from vanity to profit was nothing less than the power of divine grace.

Watchman Nee, *A Table in the Wilderness,* June 27

We must take note that Jacob always gave God the credit for anything good that happened to him. See Genesis 31:1–16, 42; 32:9–12; 35:3; 48:11, 15–16. People think of Jacob as a troublemaker. In his disobedience, he brought trouble to himself; but God used him to bless others. He blessed Laban (Gen. 30:27–30), Pharaoh (Gen. 47:7, 10), his twelve sons (Gen. 49), and Joseph's sons (Gen. 48). God had blessed Jacob (Gen. 32:29; 35:9) and he blessed others (see Gen. 12:1–3).

WWW

"The elder shall serve the younger" (Gen. 25:23; Rom. 9:10–13). God often bypassed the firstborn and chose the second-born: Abel, not Cain; Isaac, not Ishmael; Jacob, not Esau; Ephraim, not Manasseh. David was the eighth son in Jesse's family, but God made David His firstborn (Ps. 89:3, 27). God rejects our first birth and accepts only the second birth. "You must be born again" (John 3:7).

WWW

Jacob was "a plain man" (Gen. 25:27 KJV), "peaceful" (NASB), "quiet" (NIV).

WWW

Let us keep this in mind, that although Jacob had all these failings, God was with him, and blessed him, and condescended to call himself the God of Jacob, the God of Israel; and this all magnifies grace. . . . Oh, may God help us to learn a lesson from Jacob; and may we know what it is to put ourselves wholly in God's hands, and let God plan for us.

D. L. Moody, *The Gospel Awakening,* p. 626

Primarily, this man's life story is a revelation of the patience of God. . . . The central lesson is the revelation of the value of faith, however fearful it is.

GCM, *26 Sermons,* 3:96

Jacob . . . has so many points of contact with ourselves. . . . His *failings* speak to us. . . . His aspirations speak to us. . . . His sorrows speak to us.

Meyer, *Israel,* pp. 12–13

Genesis 28–31

God revealed Jacob to himself. He might have gone on for years in dreary self-content, ignorant of the evils that lurked within his heart.

Meyer, *Israel,* p. 56

Jesus identified Himself with Jacob's ladder (John 1:43–51).

Isaac believed Jacob was Esau, and Jacob believed Leah was Rachel.

WWW

O what a tangled web we weave
When first we practice to deceive.

Sir Walter Scott

He works for seven years for his wife, and then gets another woman in her place. He had started out wrong with a lie on his lips (Gen. 27:18–24), and now he gets paid back in his own coin.

Moody, *Words, Work, and Workers,* p. 162

No marriage is heaven-made, heaven-sent or heaven-sanctioned, which does not spring from a supreme love. Alas, how many marry from some less worthy motive!

Meyer, Israel, p. 67

Speaking generally, I should say that Leah had the keys of Jacob's house, Rachel the keys of Jacob's heart. Leah seems to have influenced his judgment; Rachel never ceased to hold his love.

GM-RWB, p. 115

Peniel (Genesis 32)

At Bethel, God met Jacob in tenderness and encouragement, even though he had sinned against his father and his brother. God assured him and promised to care for him. It was not at Bethel but at Peniel that God wrestled with Jacob. First he blesses us, then he breaks us. It is the goodness of God that leads us to repentance (Rom. 2:4).

WWW

Is not this the key to God's dealing with us all? He brings us into sore straits; He shuts us up in a corner. . . . At such moments there is only one resource left. It is Himself! We must fly to God to escape from God.

Meyer, Israel, p. 96

It is a strange thing how often in the Bible you find that, far from healing people, God crippled them. He crippled Jacob, so that even though he was renamed Israel, "a prince with God," he "halted upon his thigh" from the day he met and wrestled with God.

Redpath, Making of a Man, p. 190

"What is your name?" (Gen. 32:27). The last time Jacob answered that question, he lied and claimed to be Esau (Gen. 27:18–19). Now he told the truth and God blessed him because he did.

WWW

He who limps is still walking.

He had abandoned the posture of defense and resistance and had
fastened himself on to the Angel—as a terrified child clasps its arms
tightly around its father's neck. That is a glad moment in the history of the human spirit when it throws both arms around the risen
Savior, and hangs on Him, and will not let Him go. It is the attitude
of blessing. It is the position of power.

> Meyer, *Israel*, p. 102

As the years go on, we begin to cling where once we struggled.

> Meyer, *Israel*, p. 104

This passage [Jacob's wrestling] is often quoted as an instance
of Jacob's earnestness in prayer. It is nothing of the sort. It is an
instance of God's earnestness to take from us all that hinders our
truest life, while we resist Him with all our might and main. [Ear-
nest prayer is sometimes pictured by the metaphor of wrestling.
See Col. 4:12 NIV.]

> Meyer, *Israel*, pp. 99–100

Genesis 33–50

I think the trouble with a great many people is that they have gone
down to Shechem instead of going to Bethel.

> Moody, *Words, Work, and Workers*, p. 164

Jacob pitched his tent *before the city*. Are not many Christians doing
so still? They live on the edge of the world, just on the borderland;
far enough away to justify a religious profession, yet near enough
to run into it for sweets.

> Meyer, *Israel*, p. 110

And Lot pitched his tent toward Sodom.

> Genesis 13:12

The birth of Benjamin was a very special blessing, but Jacob's latter years brought him many trials. His favorite wife Rachel died and also her nurse Deborah (Gen. 35). His son Reuben defiled his father's bed (35:22; see 49:4), and Judah committed sin with his daughter-in-law, Tamar (Gen. 38). His father Isaac died (35:27–29). All of this preceded the long struggle Joseph had with his brothers and the sorrow Jacob felt for twenty-two years because he thought Joseph was dead.

WWW

When it came to Joseph's years in Egypt, Jacob and Joseph had two different viewpoints. Not knowing that Joseph was alive, Jacob said, "All these things are against me!" (Gen. 42:36), when actually everything was working *for* him (Rom. 8:28). Looking back on his own experiences, Joseph said to his brothers, "You meant it for evil, but God meant it for good" (Gen. 50:20).

WWW

Abraham went down to Egypt against the will of God and brought trouble (Gen. 12), but Jacob went to Egypt in the will of God and brought blessing (Gen. 46:1–4).

[Genesis 48:1–7] Two places and two persons crowd out everything else from his vision—Bethel, where God appeared to him, and Ephrath, where Rachel was taken from him. Faith and love—a great religious blessing and a tender earthly happiness—have made him the man he is and sum up his life.

Strahan, *Hebrew Ideals,* p. 337

Note how often the name *Israel* is used instead of *Jacob* (Gen. 48:8, 10, 11, 14).

Genesis 49 is both a prophecy (v. 1) and a blessing (v. 28). The old father let some skeletons out of the closet and revealed the consequences of family sins. The three eldest sons—Reuben, Simeon, and Levi—are written down as failures (vv. 3–7). Reuben was guilty of a sin of the flesh and lost the blessing of the firstborn. He was replaced by Joseph, who was Jacob's firstborn by Rachel. Simeon and Levi were guilty of anger and violence and were replaced by Joseph's two sons Ephraim and Manasseh.

WWW

Hebrews 11:21 says two things about Jacob's death: he blessed his sons and he leaned on his staff. He was a pilgrim to the very end! See Genesis 32:10 and 47:9. Death is the last test of our faith, and if we have walked as pilgrims with the Lord, we will be triumphant.

WWW

Jacob's funeral (Gen. 50:10–11) must have been a strong witness to the people of the pagan nations in the area. How believers die and are buried is indeed their last witness.

WWW

He had touched me in the seat of my natural strength and now, broken and shattered through solitary confinement with every-thing gone, my work, my liberty, my Bible, and now it seemed life itself, I could only cling to him for his blessing. I would no doubt never be the same again. Then like a shaft of light in the mind, the relevance of Jacob's act of faith in Hebrews, where he is seen leaning on his staff in worship. . . . What does it matter if I come up from the waters limping? What does it matter if I am never the same again, provided my name is Israel? Then as a prince with God, having no confidence in the flesh, will I lean on my staff for my lameness and worship 'til the day dawn and the shadows flee away. . . . I remembered that God's Word said that, as Jacob passed over Penuel, the sun rose upon him. So after this, I viewed everything as walking into the dawning, going on into the golden daybreak and the morning without a cloud.

Geoffrey T. Bull, *When Iron Gates Yield*
(London: Hodder & Stoughton, 1976), p. 188

Jeremiah

Babylon is mentioned over two hundred times in Jeremiah's prophecy. The word *sword* is used seventy-one times. But the key word is *heart*, used seventy-five times. Jeremiah is preeminently "the prophet of the heart." His messages reveal his own heart as well as the heart of God. "Though the story of his life is fragmentary," wrote Hugh Black, "we can read the story of his heart. . . . We see a timid, shrinking man in process of hardening to be made the prophet required for his generation" (*Listening to God,* 277). Judah was a backslidden nation (Jer. 2:19; 3:6, 8, 11, 12, 22; 5:6; 8:5; 14:7; Lam. 1:14; 3:27), and Jeremiah called the rulers, priests, and people to return to the Lord. The prophet uses the word *travail* to describe the coming judgment (4:31; 6:24; 13:21; 22:23; 30:6; 49:34; 50:43), a word of pain but also a word of hope; for the woman in travail joyfully brings forth new life into the world (John 16:20–22). It was not Judah's exile in Babylon that broke Jeremiah's heart but Judah's sins that demanded the exile. God can bring his people back to their land, but God can't force them to return to him. Jeremiah was a quiet and retiring man who was pushed into the trenches, and he depended much on prayer (Jer. 7:16; 11:14, 18–20; 12:1–4, 11; 15:10, 15–18; 17:14–18; 18:19–23; 20:7–11, 14–18).

WWW

You made much of your own weakness, now what are you going to make of God's strength? . . . Get into the irreligious habit of measuring everything by your own resources; of asking whether you are personally equal to this or that task; and in all probability you will cower in abject fear before the burden and servitude of life; but get into the contrary habit—the habit of setting God always at your right hand, and of being sure that Right must prevail, that the helping angels never tire, that though God's mill grinds slow, it grinds exceeding small; fix these great things in your heart, and then up the steepest road you will walk with a firm step, and the coldest night-wind will neither shorten nor trouble your song.

Joseph Parker, *The Ark of God,* pp. 173–74

The task of the prophet is not to smooth things over but to make things right.

Eugene Peterson, *Run with the Horses,* p. 89

Are you going to live cautiously or courageously?

Peterson, *Run with the Horses,* p. 18

Life is a continuous exploration of ever more reality. Life is a constant battle against everyone and everything that corrupts or diminishes its reality. . . . Some people as they grow up become less. . . . Other people as they grow up become more. . . . Always [Jeremiah] was pushing out the borders of reality, exploring new territory. And always he was vigorous in battle, challenging and contesting the shoddy, the false, the vile.

Peterson, *Run with the Horses,* p. 24

I am tired of hearing the words "I can't." Jeremiah said, "I am a child"; but the Lord didn't pat him on the back and say, "Jeremiah, that is very good. I like that in you; your humility is beautiful." Oh, no! God didn't want any such mock humility. He reproved and rebuked it. I do not like the humility that is too humble to do what it is bid. When my children are too humble to do as they are bid, I pretty soon find some way to make them; I say, "Go and do it!" The Lord wants us to "go and do it."

Catherine Booth, *They Said It,* p. 56

[Jeremiah 12:5] There is no attempt at explanation. God never explains Himself in a ready-made fashion. God explains Himself through life. God explains Himself by deeds. . . . The answer to the complaint against the hardness of his lot is simply the assertion that it shall be harder still.

Hugh Black, *Listening to God,* p. 231

It was the answer Jeremiah needed. He needed to be braced, not pampered. He is taught the need of endurance. . . . God appeals to the strength in Jeremiah, not to the weakness.

Black, *Listening to God,* p. 282

The prophet Jeremiah is perhaps the most misunderstood of all the Bible characters. His very name has been made a word in English, jeremiad, which means to us a tirade, and a long and tedious complaint.

Hugh Black, *According to My Gospel,* p. 95

How unjust is the common idea of the weeping prophet. It is not private sorrow, but the grief of a true patriot. Other prophets had often to speak words of hope, but his message was one of doom.

Black, *According to My Gospel*, p. 103

We are all tempted to turn to the easy ways of escaping the burden [Jer. 9:2]. We can learn from Jeremiah the paramount claims of duty. Learn to give up all the undisciplined desires and unchastened dreams after self-satisfaction. Learn to submit personal inclinations to the great call to be true to God and the right.

Black, *According to My Gospel,* p. 103

Life demands from you the strength you possess. Only one feat is possible—not to have run away.

Hammarskjöld, *Markings*, p. 8

Ah, if you knew what peace there is in an accepted sorrow!

Madame Guyon

Jeremiah was not allowed to have a wife (Jer. 16:1–4), for he was a sign that there was no future for that generation, for they rejected God. Hosea's wife proved unfaithful to him and he had to buy her back out of the shameful slave market, a sign that God would not abandon his people. Ezekiel's wife was taken from him in death (Ezek. 24:15–27) and he was forbidden to show public sorrow. God would destroy Jerusalem and the temple because Judah deserved to be punished, and the people should not mourn.

WWW

Job

The theme of Job is not "Why do the righteous suffer?" The theme of Job is "Do the righteous believe that God is worth suffering for?" Satan's challenge to the Lord was that Job was a godly man only because God had blessed him. It was part of the bargain: "You bless me and I will obey you." But Job's faith in God was much deeper than Satan imagined. Although Job uttered some impetuous words, he did not sin as did his three friends and Elihu, and the Lord told Job to pray for them! The Lord affirmed that Job was a godly man, and so did Ezekiel (14:14, 20). It was Satan who slandered his character and God who defended it.

WWW

They [Job's three friends] plead a poor cause well, while Job pleads a good cause poorly.

John Calvin

It is faith's work to claim and challenge lovingkindness out of all the rough strokes of God.

Samuel Rutherford

I had a million questions to ask God: but when I met Him, they all fled my mind, and it didn't seem to matter. [See Job 23:3–4; 31:35.]

Christopher Morley

Be silent about great things; let them grow inside you.

Baron Friedrich von Hugel

As one grows older and gains a little wisdom one increasingly hesitates to give advice. Probably the hidden reason for that hesitancy is that advice implies seniority. Nobody really wants to be impertinent, and, unless there is real love and understanding, advice is apt to savor of impertinence. When Job was prosperous and wealthy, we do not hear of his friends offering advice. They kept that for the days when he was wretched, and the glory of his prosperity had vanished. The most irritating thing about these men is not the bland assumption of their arguments, it is their assumption of superiority. One could tell that the disciples were young men by their great readiness to give advice. They did not hesitate to advise the Lord Himself.

GHM, *The Gateways of the Stars*, p. 244

The Book of Job is not strictly a pessimistic book. It does not despair of the universe—spite of all its sorrows! What it does despair of is the adequacy of any one of man's existing theories, or all of these theories united, to furnish a *solution* of its sorrows.

GM-RMB, 1:351

Now, observe carefully why the Book of Job rejects old theories of the origins of pain. It has because it has found a new theory. All the former ones had explained suffering as the result of defect in the *creature*. Here, the bold view is advanced that it had its origin in a need felt by the Creator—the Divine need for love. . . . "Oh!" cries Satan, "nobody loves you for *yourself*, not even Job! You have made it worthwhile to serve you." . . . Satan has put his hand upon a real weakness—[man's] association of Divine love with temporal rewards.

GM-RMB, 1:352–53

His friends wanted to *rob* him of his patience—to take away his power to *wait without a reason.*

GM-RMB, 1:360

In fact Job has not received any logical answers to the precise questions which he asked. . . . For God's answer is not an idea, a proposition, like the conclusion of a theorem; it is Himself. He revealed Himself to Job; Job found personal contact with Him (Job 42:1).

Paul Tournier, *Guilt and Grace,* p. 86

John the Baptist

Like Jeremiah and Ezekiel, he was a priest called to be a prophet. Jeremiah announced the new covenant (Jer. 31:31ff), Ezekiel described the new temple (Ezek. 40–48), and John pointed to the new sacrifice, the Lamb of God (John 1:29). John had the special privilege of introducing the Messiah to the nation. John was a voice, but Jesus is the Word (John 1:1–4, 23); John was the best man, but Jesus is the Bridegroom (John 3:27–30); John was a lamp but Jesus is the Light of the World (John 5:35; 8:12). Before he was born, John rejoiced in Jesus (Luke 1:39–45); in life, he pointed to Jesus (John 1:29); and after death he brought people to Jesus (John 10:40–42). And all this without performing a single miracle!

WWW

John was also a road-builder, a trail-blazer (Isa. 40:3; Matt. 3:1–3). He prepared and announced the way for God and sinners to come together. That is the purpose of our witness, to clear the way so sinners can come home to God.

WWW

John was not a reed blowing in the wind (Luke 7:25). The "winds of doctrine" did not sway him (Eph. 4:14).

John sought no honor among men. It was his delight to say concerning our Lord Jesus, "He must increase, but I must decrease" (John 3:30). . . . A man is not to be estimated according to his rank but according to his character.

CHS, 26:401

The very spirit of the Christian ministry consists in those blessed words, "He must increase, but I must decrease." I fulfill my course, it will soon be done, I point to Christ.

F. W. Robertson, *Sermons,* 5:150

Think of this! Thirty years' preparation for one year's work.

F. W. Robertson, *Sermons,* 5:258

What he had learned in the desert was contained in a few words— Reality lies at the root of religious life. . . . Personal reformation, personal reality, *that* was John's message to the world.

F. W. Robertson, *Sermons on Biblical Subjects,* p. 149

John laid the axe to the root of the trees (Matt. 3:10). He was a radical. The English word *radical* comes from the Latin word *radix,* meaning "root." He belonged to no religious party, he accepted no entertainment in people's homes, he catered to no politicians. He was a "loner" in the service of the Lord.

WWW

John Mark. *See* Mark

Jonah

There is no worse enemy, nor one more troublesome to the soul, than you are to yourself, if you are not in harmony with the Spirit.

Thomas à Kempis

We may never plead providential arrangement as an excuse for doing wrong. . . . [Jonah] walks on the quay, and the first thing he sees is a ship going to Tarshish! . . . I pray you never blaspheme God by laying your sins on the back of His providence.

CHS, 36:597

Jonah saw God's will as punishment. Jesus saw God's will as nourishment (John 4:34).

WWW

It is what Jonah does that is important, not so much what he says. In chapter 1, he is a "prodigal son" who wanted to flee to the far country and avoid obeying God's will. In chapter 2, he prays for forgiveness and restoration, and God graciously grants his requests. In chapters 3 and 4, he is an "elder brother" who grudgingly obeys and then sits outside the city hoping for judgment to fall! Yet in all this, he is a "sign" of the resurrection of Jesus Christ, the one greater than Jonah (Matt. 12:39–41).

WWW

According to Jonah chapter 1, everything cooperated with the
Lord except Jonah—the wind and the sea, the great fish, and even
the heathen sailors. Jonah would not try to rescue the pagan city
of Nineveh from destruction, but the unconverted sailors tried to
rescue Jonah. Yet Jonah was the cause of their peril!

WWW

God is in our comforts, for He prepared a plant to shade Jonah
(4:5–6). God is in our bereavements and losses, for He prepared
a worm to destroy the plant (4:7). God is in our severest trials, for
He prepared a vehement wind to make Jonah miserable (4:8).

Adapted from CHS, 43:75

Read Father Mapple's sermon on Jonah in chapter 8 of *Moby Dick*
by Herman Melville.

Joseph

Why did Jacob have a special love for Joseph? Joseph was born
to Jacob in his old age (Gen. 37:3), the son of his favorite wife
Rachel, and no doubt Joseph inherited her beauty (Gen. 29:17;
39:6). When Jacob looked at Joseph, he saw Rachel. But certainly
Jacob detected a mature spiritual quality in Joseph that was lacking
in the older sons, and Jacob suspected that God had something
special in store for the boy. When Joseph shared his dreams with
the family, Jacob did not understand them but he did ponder
them (Gen. 37:11). Joseph's special garment elevated him above
the other sons as though he were the firstborn in charge of the
estate, but this only motivated the brothers to envy him (Gen.
37:3–4, 11; Acts 7:9) and hate him (Gen. 37:5, 8). "Will you be
firstborn and rule over us?" They sold him, and what God had
planned came to pass. They meant it for evil, but God meant it
for good (Gen. 50:20). The dreams that God gave to Joseph were
the assurance that one day he would reign. But dreams without
disciplines become nightmares, so God sent Joseph to Egypt to
serve and to suffer for thirteen years (Matt. 25:23).

WWW

[Genesis 37:2] He [Joseph] was jealous for the family name, which they had already "made to stink among the inhabitants of the land" (Gen. 34:30).

F. B. Meyer, *Joseph*, p. 14

Reuben saved Joseph's life (Gen. 37:21), but because of his sin Reuben still lost the birthright (Gen. 49:3–4), which went to Joseph through his sons Ephraim and Manasseh (1 Chron. 5:1–2). Reuben was Leah's firstborn and Joseph was Rachel's firstborn. Laban's scheme to give Leah first place was overruled by the Lord.

Scripture frequently sums up a man's life in a single sentence. Here is the biography of Joseph sketched by inspiration. . . . "The Lord was with Joseph." [See Gen. 39:2–3, 21, 23; 41:38; Acts 7:9.]

CHS, 27:413

Reputation is what others suppose we are; character is what God knows we really are. Reputation is what is chiseled on your tombstone. Character is what the angels say about you before the throne of God. Joseph's character is summed up in Romans 12:11–12. Joseph fled (Gen. 39:12; 2 Tim. 2:22). He lost his coat but he kept his character.

In Bondage (Genesis 39–40; see also Psalm 105:18)

Joseph's temptation came when all was going well, and it came from an unexpected source. It was repeated (Gen. 39:10) and, because nobody was present, to give in seemed "safe." To yield would have given Joseph a strong ally in Potiphar's wife, but it would have ruled out the blessing of God.

Summarized from Theodore Epp, *Joseph*, pp. 38–41

Evil may have temporary victories, but remember that they are only temporary. We must wait quietly; we must go forward humbly.

Epp, *Joseph*, p. 56

If you are now going through testing, there are three things you should especially remember. First, God's way is the wisest way. . . . God trains us through chastening. Second, God's time is the best time. God was working out His purpose through Joseph. Third, God's grace is sufficient. The secret of waiting *for* God is waiting *on* God.

Summarized from Epp, Joseph, pp. 65–66

When he told his story, Joseph did not implicate his brothers. He told the prisoners that he had been "stolen" (Gen. 40:15 KJV).

God wants iron saints, and since there is no way of imparting iron to the moral nature than by letting His people suffer, He lets us suffer.

Meyer, Joseph, p. 55

It is in the prison that Joseph is fitted for the unknown life of Pharaoh's palace, and if he could have foreseen the future, he would not have wondered at the severe discipline.

Meyer, Joseph, p. 56

Whenever you get into a prison of circumstances, be on the watch. Prisons are rare places for seeing things. . . . The night is the time to see the stars.

Meyer, Joseph, p. 58

How to act in prison: Don't be surprised at your suffering; don't be weary in well-doing; don't avenge yourself but let God vindicate you.

Summarized from Meyer, Joseph, pp. 60-61

In all the discipline of life it is of the utmost importance to see but one ordaining overruling will. If we view our imprisonments and misfortunes as the result of human malevolence, our lives will be filled with fret and unrest. It is hard to suffer wrong at the hands of man, and to think that perhaps it might never have been. But there is a truer and more restful view, to consider all things as being under the law and rule of God; so that though they may originate in and come to us through the spite and malice of our fellows, yet, since before they reach us they have had to pass through the environing [encircling] atmosphere of the Divine Presence, they have been transformed into his own sweet will for us.

Meyer, *Joseph*, p. 62

Slavery itself was a small calamity compared with that which would have happened to young Joseph had he been enslaved by wicked passions.

CHS, 27:416

Exalted (Genesis 41)

God can accomplish his divine purposes even through pagans like Pharaoh (see Isa. 44:28; 45:5; Jer. 25:9; 27:6; 43:10). God can communicate with them even in their dreams (Gen. 20:1–6; 28:12; 31:10–11, 14; 37:1–11; 40:5, 9, 16). Joseph had humbled himself under God's hand and now God would exalt him (1 Peter 5:5–7). The difficult training period was ended and now he would enter into his life ministry: saving and protecting his family so that they might become a mighty nation. His first challenge would be to store up the food, and his second would be to restore his brothers to God, himself, and their father.

WWW

In his new position of prosperity, Joseph resisted and repelled the natural temptation to pride and arrogance with the same thoroughness as he had the temptation of passion—he was never drawn away from his utter loyalty to God.

Epp, *Joseph*, p. 82

[Genesis 41:50–52] Joseph was a testimony to God's faithfulness. But we must also commend Joseph for his forgetfulness in forgiving his brothers for their sins, and for the fruitfulness of his life in Egypt to God's glory (see Gen. 49:22). Was Joseph too hard on his brothers? No, for thirteen years of deception had to be dealt with, and God could not bless the nation unless the founders were right with him. Their mouths needed to be stopped (Gen. 45:3; Rom. 3:19) before God could restore them.

WWW

God sometimes allows us to be treated as we have treated Him, so that we may see our offense in its true character, and may be obliged to turn to Him with words of genuine contrition. [See Ps. 18:24–27.]

Meyer, *Joseph,* p. 97

We little realize how much pain He is suffering as He causes us pain; or how the tender heart of our Brother is filled with grief, welling up within Him as He makes Himself strange and deals so roughly with us.

Meyer, *Joseph,* p. 91

Without the work of the Holy Spirit, they might have felt remorse but not guilt. It is not enough to feel that sin is a blunder and a mistake, but not guilt. This sense of sin, however, is the prerogative of the Holy Spirit of God. He alone can convict of sin.

Meyer, *Joseph,* pp. 88–89

Keep in mind that the longer Joseph dealt with his brothers, the longer he was kept from seeing his father whom he dearly loved and missed. But the "heart surgery" on his brothers was important for them personally and for the future of the nation.

WWW

[Genesis 42:24] God deliver me from the man who has no tears! One Man stands supreme in all history, and in all the writing that gives us the record of His life, there is no more beautiful thing than this: "Jesus wept." The capacity for tears is the last demonstration of greatness.

GCM, *26 Sermons,* 3:133

Joseph wept when he was put into the pit (Gen. 42:21–22); when he heard his brothers admit their wrongs (42:24); when he saw his brother Benjamin (43:30); when he was reconciled to them

(45:2, 14–15); when he met his father Jacob (46:29); when his father died (50:1); and when his brothers asked for forgiveness (50:15–21).

Jacob's outlook and actions changed when he heard that Joseph was alive, and he wanted to see him. It reminds us of the change that occurred in the first followers of Jesus when they heard that he was alive.

WWW

[Genesis 47:7] Joseph was not ashamed of his aged father, 130 years old. Jacob walked with a limp and leaned on his staff, but he was a prince with God and the source of the salvation of all Egypt. Jacob was not impressed with Pharaoh but showed his faith by blessing him (Heb. 7:7).

WWW

[Genesis 49:22–26] In the images he used of Joseph in his dying prophecy, Jacob revealed the secret of Joseph's life. Joseph was a fruitful bough, a branch in the vine (John 15:1–8), and he drew strength from a hidden spring (Ps. 1:3). During his prison days, Joseph experienced the pruning of the Lord that prepared him for the throne. He also experienced persecution and opposition from family and acquaintances, but he triumphed over it all. God was his strength, his shepherd, and his rock of refuge, and it was the blessing of God that caused him to prosper. Joseph's faithfulness took him "over the wall" and brought life to Egypt and blessing to the whole world, for "salvation is of the Jews" (John 4:22).

WWW

Joseph was natural and beautiful, high and noble, devoted to duty, full of sagacity; a youth dreaming dreams that indicated the future, because his life was strong and pure, and the secret of all was that he lived by the fountain, his roots taking hold of the hidden resources of power.

GCM, 26 Sermons, 3:116

Genesis 50:15–21

The petition was suggested by their own anticipations of vengeance (v. 15). Now where came these anticipations? I reply, from their own hearts. Under similar circumstances they would have acted so, and they took for granted that Joseph would. We suspect according to our nature; we look on others as we feel.

F. W. Robertson, Sermons on Biblical Subjects, p. 33

The only revenge which is essentially Christian is that of retaliating by forgiveness.

F. W. Robertson, Sermons on Biblical Subjects, p. 37

But Joseph has no thought of humiliating his brothers. He thinks only of making them better and happier men. He hastens to speak gracious words to them, lifting up their thoughts to God, on whom his own mind is habitually fixed. Remorse has done its work. Let them now look away from themselves and their sin to the God who is behind all events, and who guides and controls all human affairs, who has been overruling all his and their actions for their common good.

Strahan, Hebrew Ideals, pp. 324–25

It is very sweet as life passes by to be able to look back on dark and mysterious events and to trace the hand of God where once we saw only the malice and cruelty of men.

Meyer, Joseph, p. 28

Death (Gen. 50:24–26)

What is the glory of the eventide? It is that vision of the past that discovers God's ways, and is enabled to rejoice over our victories. It is that vision of the future which is absolutely assured of the fulfillment of God's purpose and of the completion of our work.

GCM, 26 Sermons, 3:148

"I die, but God will surely . . ." (Gen. 50:24 KJV). God buries his workers but continues his work.

The death of a man of God is not the end of his service even in this world. The coffin in Egypt was there . . . for at least two hundred years.

GCM, 26 Sermons, 3:158

Joseph knew what he believed and where he belonged. At the exodus, the Jewish people took Joseph's coffin with them and it was eventually buried in Canaan (Exod. 13:19; Josh. 24:32; Heb. 11:22). Both in their sufferings in Egypt and in their wilderness wanderings, the Jews received encouragement from this witness, for Joseph reminded them of God's promises to Abraham (Gen. 15:13–16). The believer's source of hope today is not a coffin with a corpse but an empty tomb!

WWW

Lasting Lessons

1. God has a purpose for every life.
2. A purpose for every life calls for discipline as a means of preparation.
3. The duty of life is faithfulness.
4. God will perform to the end what He has begun.
5. God is glorified when others are faithfully served.
6. God proves Himself to those who trust Him.
7. God's wisdom is verified by the outcome of events.

Summarized from Epp, Joseph, pp. 83–84

Joseph's life illustrates our divine heirship, that we are heirs of God. The Bible teaches clearly what the prerequisites of heirship are. In particular, spiritual heirship is preceded by suffering. Suffering always precedes glory (Rom. 8:16–17).

Epp, Joseph, p. 8

The doctrine of the Gospel is not simply that after dark the light comes, but that the garment which at night we call dark is that which in the morning we pronounce luminous. "Your sorrow shall be *turned into joy*" (John 16:21). It is the transformation of sorrow rather than the abolition of sorrow that is contemplated. . . . It has become a simple matter of history that Christ has triumphed by the very steps which were taken to defeat Him.

GM-RMB, 1:177

Pure optimism is not the belief that all will come right; it is the belief that all is right *now,* that nothing has ever been wrong.

GM-RMB, 1:179

In Joseph we see one who is "more than conqueror" (Rom. 8:37). He overcame the pampering of a doting father, the hatred and envy of his older brothers, the shame and pain of slavery, the temptations of the flesh, the injustice of false accusation, the humiliation of prison, the dangers of honor and power, and the human desires to get even with those who hurt him.

WWW

Joseph illustrates the truth of Romans 8:28–29. God did make all things work together for good for Joseph, and this fulfilled his purpose in making Joseph like Jesus Christ, "conformed to the image of his Son." Though nowhere in Scripture is Joseph called a type of Christ, the comparisons are too many to be accidental. Both were especially loved by their fathers, both were hated by their brethren, both were promised thrones, and both were plotted against by their enemies. Joseph and Jesus were each sold for the price of a slave and both were servants. Both were lied about and falsely accused and both were made to suffer unjustly. Both were tempted and were victorious. Joseph was with two offenders, one of whom died and the other lived, and Jesus was crucified between two offenders, one of whom trusted him and the other did not. Both were humiliated but eventually exalted. Joseph received a wife during his time of separation from his brethren, and Jesus today is taking to himself a bride. Joseph sold material bread to the world, while Jesus gives spiritual bread to the world. Neither

Joseph nor Jesus was recognized by their brethren the first time. Joseph was recognized the second time (Acts 7:13), and so will the Lord Jesus be made known to his brethren when he returns again. As Joseph's brethren and all Egypt bowed before him, so every knee will bow at the revelation of Jesus Christ.

WWW

Joseph of Arimathea (John 19:38–42)

It appears that Joseph and Nicodemus were together in their faith in Jesus Christ. We think of a "secret disciple" as a coward, but perhaps they were "secreted disciples," hidden by the Lord so that they might perform an important task—the proper burial of the body of Jesus. It was important that Jesus' body have a legitimate burial so that the miracle of the resurrection might be evident. To have a tomb prepared near Calvary indicates that they knew Jesus would die by crucifixion. To have a hundred pounds of myrrh and aloes ready in the tomb proves that they expected it to happen on Passover. Their study of the Old Testament Scriptures (see John 7:50–53) would tell them that Jesus was the Lamb of God (Exod. 12; Isa. 53) who would die on a cross (Ps. 22). When they touched the dead body of Jesus, they were defiled and could not partake of the Passover feast; but this did not upset them. They knew the true Lamb of God! They lost their unbelieving friends who served with them on the Jewish council, but they entered into the fellowship of the children of God. Both men were wealthy, but their wealth meant nothing compared to the privilege of knowing their Messiah (Phil. 3:7–10).

WWW

Joshua

He was born into slavery in Egypt, where he also may have learned how to be a military man. Moses chose him to be the leader of the army of Israel, thus preparing him for his task of conquering the Promised Land. Joshua was Moses' servant and then became his successor. He ruled over the Jewish people until his death and was succeeded by a series of judges who ruled in various parts of the land. He is a type of Jesus Christ, who has conquered the enemy for us and will lead us into our spiritual inheritance if we will trust him and obey him (Heb. 1–4). The three geographic locations in Joshua's life—Egypt, the wilderness, and Canaan—speak to us today of three spiritual conditions: Egypt—the world with its bondage; the wilderness—the life of unbelief and disobedience; Canaan—the rest and riches of our spiritual inheritance. Only Caleb and Joshua survived the wilderness journey and entered the Promised Land, because they believed God and did not rebel against him.

WWW

Joshua was the successor of Moses in certain senses. There are ways in which Joshua could not succeed Moses, as there are always ways in which no one man can succeed another. That is an important principle. I wish we always remembered that in the work of the Christian Church. There are things which only the one man can do, and no man can carry on exactly upon the lines of his predecessor. There were things Joshua could not do, but they were mainly things which Moses had done. It is equally true that Moses could not do what Joshua was appointed to do. Again, Moses' work was incomplete without Joshua; and Joshua's work would have been impossible but for that of Moses.

G. Campbell Morgan, from a sermon preached at Tabernacle
Presbyterian Church, Philadelphia, PA, 1931

None of us can tell for what God is educating us. We fret and murmur at the narrow round and daily task of ordinary life, not realizing that it is only thus that we can be prepared for the high and holy office which awaits us. We must descend before we can ascend.

F. B. Meyer, *Joshua and the Land of Promise,* p. 19

The supreme enquiry for each of us, when summoned to a new work, is—not whether we possess sufficient strength or qualification for it, but—if we have been called to it of God; and when that is so, there is no further cause for anxiety.

Meyer, *Joshua*, pp. 20–21

Courage is necessary to succeed in Christian work. I have yet to find a man who is easily discouraged that amounts to anything anywhere. . . . God hasn't any use for a man who is all the time looking on the dark side.

Moody, *Words, Work, and Workers*, p. 167

Joshua was very highly favored in the matter of promises. The promises given to him by God were broadly comprehensive and exceedingly encouraging. But Joshua was not therefore to say within himself, "These covenant arrangements will surely be fulfilled, and I may therefore sit still and do nothing." On the contrary, because God had decreed that the land should be conquered, Joshua was to be diligent to lead the people onward to battle. He was not to use the promise as a couch upon which his indolence might luxuriate, but as a girdle wherewith to gird up his loins for future activity. As a spur to energy, let us always regard the gracious promises of our God.

CHS, 14:97

Obedience is the highest practical courage.

CHS, 14:98

New dangers will bring new protections; new difficulties, new helps; new discouragements, new comforts; so that we may rejoice in tribulations also, because there are so many newly-opened doors of God's mercy to us.

CHS, 21:49

No Scripture is of private interpretation; no text has spent itself upon the person who first received it. God's comforts are like wells, which no one man or set of men can drain dry, however mighty may be their thirst. . . . The fountain of our text first gushed forth to refresh Joshua, but if we are in Joshua's position, and are of his character, we may bring our water-pots and fill them to the brim.

CHS, 21:52

We cannot live upon tradition; we cannot be courageous because of something which happened to other people: there must be personal contact with divine realities, an individual touch, a present and indestructible consciousness of God's nearness and of the reality of things; then there will be courage and testimony and service and sacrifice.

Parker, *The People's Bible*, 5:326

God's promise was, "I will drive out the enemy!" (See Josh. 3:10; 13:13; 14:12; 17:13; 23:5.) But God gave the same promises through Moses. (See Exod. 6:1; 11:1; 23:28–31; 33:2; 34:11, 24; Lev. 18:24; 20:23; Num. 22:6, 11; 33:52; Deut. 4:27, 38; 7:17, 22; 9:3–5; 11:23; 18:12; 33:27.)

[Joshua 5:12] You are the successor to Moses, the great miracle-worker, and one of the first things that happens is that the manna ceases—the end of a daily miracle! How did the people respond to this? As they marched through Canaan, they were to eat what the land produced. Was God's provision of seasonal food any less a miracle than the daily manna?

WWW

[Joshua 5:13–15] Not until we take the place of a servant can He take His place as Lord.

Watchman Nee

Joshua learned that he was second in command!

WWW

The vessels which are meet for the Master's use are pure ones. Cleanness, rather than cleverness, is the prime condition of successful service.

Meyer, *Joshua*, p. 66

Note the name "the Lord of Hosts." The Lord of the armies! (See Gen. 32:1–2; 2 Kings 6:15–17; 1 Sam. 17:45; Ps. 34:7; 46:7, 11; Isa. 40:26.)

[Joshua 3:5] The wonders of tomorrow depend on the sanctification of today.

GHM, Highways of the Heart, p. 2

[Joshua 6] We are apt to fight the world with weapons borrowed from its arsenals, and adopt methods which savor rather of the flesh than of the Spirit. It is a great mistake. Our only hope is to act on strictly spiritual lines, because we wrestle not with flesh and blood.

Meyer, Joshua, p. 74

[Joshua 7–8] Twice Joshua ran ahead of the Lord and did not wait for orders—when he attacked Ai and when he made a covenant with the Gibeonites (Josh. 9). Both led to shameful and discouraging defeat. But God enabled Joshua to use the defeat at Ai to conquer the enemy, and he made his mistake with the Gibeonites "work for him" and assigned the Gibeonites to be servants in the camp. If you make a mistake, make it work for you!

WWW

There is nothing small in the Christian life—nothing so small that we can combat in our own strength. Apart from God the smallest temptation will be more than a match for us.

Meyer, Joshua, p. 79

Ah, if Joshua had only prostrated himself amid the shoutings of victory over Jericho, there would have been no need for him to prostrate himself amid the outcry of a panic-stricken host.

Meyer, Joshua, p. 81

God uses different strategies, not only to confuse the enemy but also to strengthen our faith, lest we depend on methods and experience instead of depending on the Lord. At Jericho, the army was in the open, but at Ai, the soldiers were hidden in ambush. The victory at Jericho was a miracle of God; the victory at Ai was a victory of strategy from God. The army was forbidden to take spoil at Jericho but encouraged to do so at Ai. If Achan had waited just a few days, he could have taken what he wanted and saved his life.

WWW

Life, like war, is a series of mistakes, and he is not the best Christian nor the best general, who makes the fewest false steps. He is the best who wins the most splendid victories by the retrieval of mistakes. Forget mistakes; organize victories out of mistakes.

F. W. Robertson, *Sermons,* 1:66

Judas Iscariot

His name comes from "Judah" and means "praise" (Gen. 29:35). He ruined a good name; nobody today would call a son Judas. Iscariot means "man of Kerioth," a city in Judah (Josh. 15:25), seventeen miles south of Hebron. His father's name was Simon (John 6:71). Judas was the only apostle who did not come from Galilee. He is called the *betrayer* (Matt. 10:4; Mark 3:19; John 13:21; 18:2), the *traitor* (Luke 6:16), a *devil* (John 6:70), a *thief* (John 12:6), the *son of perdition* (John 17:2–12), and the *guide* (Acts 1:16). Jesus knew from the beginning that Judas was not a believer and would betray him (John 2:24–25; 6:64–71). Judas was not clean (John 13:10–11) and had not been "chosen" (John 13:18). The indication seems to be that Judas was a counterfeit rather than an apostate (Matt. 7:21–23). Note that there was another Judas in the apostolic band (Luke 6:16; John 14:22) and that Jesus had a half-brother named Judas (Matt.13:55) who wrote the Epistle of Jude. Judas ministered in preaching and healing just as the other apostles did (Matt. 10:1ff; Mark 6:7–13), and they had no idea he would be a traitor. The Old Testament background is Psalms 41:9; 55:12–14; and 69:25; and see Acts 1:15–20. Note also Ahithophel in 2 Samuel 15 and 17.

Judas was not the victim of "prophetic determinism"—somebody had to betray Jesus, so Judas was chosen, and what he did benefited all mankind. Judas was not an innocent hero. He could have been a true disciple had he made the right choices. He heard Jesus preach, he saw him perform miracles, and he knew the truth, yet he rejected it. At the same time, Judas was not called as a witness at the trial of Jesus! His last confession was that he had "betrayed innocent blood" (Matt. 27:4). It is difficult to untangle the motives that drove him. Did he want Jesus to overthrow Rome and establish the Jewish kingdom? Was he disappointed in Jesus' approach to ministry, caring for the poor and needy and condemning the Jewish leaders? At the Last Supper, Jesus made every attempt to rescue Judas, but Judas would not submit. Jesus protected Judas from the other disciples and did not openly expose his wickedness. He welcomed Judas with a kiss and gave him the place of honor next to himself. Jesus even washed Judas's feet! Had Peter known the truth about Judas, he might have used his sword!

WWW

More is told of Judas in the Gospels than of any other disciple except Peter. Yet he is little known; indeed, he is wrapped in mystery.

S. Pearce Carey, *Jesus and Judas,* p. 7

That He chose Judas as one of them [the disciples] was the highest tribute He could pay him; and if he was, as is so widely believed, the only Judaean, the tribute was even more striking still.

Carey, *Jesus and Judas,* p. 28

They [the disciples] never dreamed that they were to be preachers. . . . They supposed themselves destined to be the servants, helpers, officers of a King, of a literal, visible, victorious, long-reigning glorious King. That Jesus was moving to Kingship was their clearest conviction. . . . Moreover, they felt assured that this Kingship was immanent.

Carey, *Jesus and Judas,* p. 33

Among the apostles, the one absolutely stunning success was Judas, and the one thoroughly groveling failure was Peter. Judas was a success in the ways that most impress us: he was successful both financially and politically. He cleverly arranged to control the money of the apostolic band; he skillfully manipulated the political forces of the day to accomplish his goal. And Peter was a failure in ways that we most dread: he was impotent in a crisis and socially inept. . . . Time, of course, has reversed our judgments on these two men. Judas is now a byword for betrayal, and Peter is one of the most honored names in church and world.

Eugene Peterson, Traveling Light, p. 95

The raw material of a devil is an angel bereft of holiness. You cannot make a Judas except out of an apostle.

CHS, 35:302

If I had any sympathetic feelings towards any character in the Old Testament, it was towards such people as Cain, Jezebel, Haman, Agag, Sisera; in the New Testament my friends, if any, were Ananias, Caiaphas, Judas and Pontius Pilate.

George Orwell

[Orwell was writing about his early school days. In later years, these may not have been his choices.]

When a man loses fellowship with God he loses power to possess anything that God gives him. Suppose the most flaming illustration of the thing in all the Bible is the story of Judas in those last and awful hours. He turned from the highest, and he sold the Highest for thirty pieces of silver.

GCM, 8:213

Of course Judas fell gradually. That's the way any man falls. Neither the heights of sainthood nor the depths of infamy are reached other than by a step at a time.

William E. Biederwolf, The Kiss of Judas and Other Sermons, p. 14

In the list of Disciples the name of Peter is mentioned first, and the name of Judas is mentioned last. They are alike in this that they both sinned grievously against their Master. . . . But there is this difference—"Peter went out and wept bitterly," and turned again to the One he had so greatly wronged. . . . But with Judas the case was different. There was remorse, but no repentance.

Biederwolf, Kiss of Judas, p. 19 [Note 2 Cor. 7:9–10]

Of course the question will arise, "Why did our Lord choose a man whom He knew to be a devil" (John 6:70)? A hard question, but there is a harder still—"Why did Jesus choose *you*?" . . . In your heart of hearts are you saying, "If this man were a prophet, he would know what manner of man this Judas is, for he is a sinner"? O thou self-contented Simon, presently the Lord will have somewhat to say unto thee, and His parable will smite thee like a sword.

Parker, *The Ark of God,* p. 43

[Parker is referring to Luke 7:36–50.]

Shall I startle you if I say that there is a still more terrible state than that of such anguish as Iscariot's? To have worn out the moral sense, to have become incapable of pain, to have the conscience seared as with a hot iron, to be "past feeling"—that is the consummation of wickedness.

Parker, *The Ark of God,* pp. 45–46

[It] must be forever true that non-existence is better than sinfulness. [Matt. 26:24; Mark 14:21.]

Parker, *The Ark of God,* p. 48

Different names affect us differently. One could not well think of John without being impressed with the power of love, nor could one consider Paul without being impressed first of all with his zeal and then with his learning. Certainly one could not study Peter without saying that his strongest characteristic was his enthusiasm. . . . But to think of Judas is to shudder.

J. Wilbur Chapman, *And Judas Iscariot,* pp. 12–13

Not only did Judas sell Jesus for thirty pieces of silver; he also sold himself.

And it is strange that on the night of the betrayal, perhaps the two loneliest figures in the world were the sinful disciple and his sinless Lord. But oh! the world of difference between the two! Christ lonely because He was the Son of God, bearing His cross alone and going out into the glory. And Judas lonely because he was the son of perdition, with every harmony destroyed by sin, and going out into the night.

GHM, *Flood-tide,* p. 202

[John 12:1–8] He [Judas] evidently judged that on the money side of things in Christ's circle, the business side, which he regarded as his own particular sphere, a trespass had been committed. So he took the lead, and made the protest. . . . He raised his voice against a sensitive woman, esteemed and loved of Christ.

Carey, *Jesus and Judas,* p. 67

[John 13:2] The Greek verb translated "put" in the KJV ("prompted" in NIV) simply means "to throw" and suggests violence. See John 8:7, 59; 15:6; 21:6. Judas had prepared the soil; now the Devil quickly and effectively planted the seed.

WWW

The religious leaders wanted to postpone the arrest of Jesus until after Passover, but God had decreed that his Son die as the Lamb of God on Passover. Unwittingly, Judas made this possible by enabling the officers to arrest Jesus privately in the garden.

"He [Judas] went immediately out, and it was night" (John 13:30 KJV). And for Judas it is still night and always will be night!

Judas kissed Jesus "effusively." (See Prov. 27:6.)

L

Lazarus (John 11–12)

We have no recorded words of Lazarus, but his "resurrection life" was such a strong witness that people believed on Jesus simply by seeing the man alive whom they knew had been dead (John 11:45; 12:9–11). See Romans 6:4.

There was no question that Jesus loved Lazarus and his sisters (John 11:3, 5, 36), yet he permitted Lazarus to get sick. He also delayed going to Bethany until Lazarus was already dead. The grief that we experience is not evidence that the Lord does not love us, and his delays are not denials of his blessing. Romans 5:8 and 8:28 are still true. Jesus had his plan and it brought glory to his name.

Jesus raised many people from the dead (Matt. 11:5), but only three of these resurrections are recorded: the daughter of Jairus (Luke 8:41–56), the son of the widow of Nain (Luke 7:11–18), and Lazarus (John 11). We have a twelve-year-old girl, a young man, and an older man, and all three were raised by the power of his word (John 5:24).

The man was wholly raised, but not wholly freed. See, here is *a living man in the garments of death!* . . . Moreover, he was *a moving man bound hand and foot.*

CHS, 30:222

121

Lot and Lot's Wife (Genesis 12–14)

There is not in the whole Bible a more instructive history than that of Lot and his family. His own history shows how the righteous scarcely are saved. His sons-in-law show well the way in which the Gospel is received by the easy careless world. His wife is a type of those who are convinced, yet never converted—who flee from the wrath to come, yet perish after all; while the angels' laying hold on the lingering family is a type of the gracious violence and sovereign mercy which God uses in delivering souls.

Robert Murray M'Cheyne, *Additional Remains,* pp. 249–50

Three "memorable" women: Lot's wife (Luke 17:32), Miriam (Deut. 24:9), and Mary of Bethany (Matt. 26:1–3).

WWW

Abraham took Lot out of Egypt but he could not take Egypt out of Lot. The Lord had the same problem with the people of Israel. "It took one night to get Israel out of Egypt but forty years to get Egypt out of Israel."

George Morrison

If there was a man under the sun that needed Abraham's counsel, and Abraham's prayers, and Abraham's influence, and to have been surrounded by the friends of Abraham, it was Lot.

D. L. Moody

Where there is one Abraham, or one David, or one Elijah, you may find a thousand Lots.

Moody, *Words, Work, and Workers,* p. 115

Lot went into Sodom with his eyes wide open. He knew he was taking his children into bad company, and bringing his household into the midst of the most abominable heathen; but the main question with him seems to have been business, business—money, money.

Moody, *Words, Work, and Workers,* p. 117

A man is spiritual when the things of the spirit are the great realities for him. A man is spiritual who lives and moves under the felt power of the unseen. A man is spiritual to whom the things of sense are but the shadows of things that are invisible, and who in every choice that he is called to immediately takes account of the unseen. The carnal man judges by the senses. The spiritual man judges by the spirit. The carnal looks at temporal advantage, the spiritual at the welfare of the soul.

GHM, *Morning Sermons,* pp. 182–83

Lot's wife was almost saved, but not quite.

CHS, 25:488

She did actually perish through sin. The first sin that she committed is that *she lingered behind.* . . . Having slackened her pace, the next thing she did was *she disbelieved.* . . . [Her] next movement [was] a direct act of rebellion: *she dared to look back.*

CHS, 25:488–89

Beware of a half-hearted religion. Beware of following Christ for any secondary motive—to please relations and friends—to keep in with the custom of the place or family in which you reside—to appear respectable and have the reputation of being religious. Follow Christ for His own sake if you follow Him at all. Be thorough, be real, be honest, be sound, be whole-hearted. If you have any religion at all, let your religion be real. See that you do not sin the *sin of Lot's wife.*

J. C. Ryle, *Holiness,* p. 173

Pharaoh saw all the miracles which Moses worked; Korah, Dathan and Abiram had heard God speaking from Mount Sinai; Hophni and Phinehas were sons of God's high priest; Saul lived in the full light of Samuel's ministry; Ahab was often warned by Elijah the prophet; Absalom enjoyed the privilege of being one of David's children; Belshazzar had Daniel the prophet hard by his door; Ananias and Sapphira joined the church in the days when the apostles were working miracles; Judas Iscariot was a chosen companion of our Lord Jesus Christ Himself. But they all sinned

with a high hand against light and knowledge; and they were all
suddenly destroyed without remedy. . . . They tell us, like Lot's
wife, that it is a perilous thing to sin against light, that God hates
sin, and that there is a hell.

Ryle, Holiness, p. 174

Lot was a good man (2 Peter 2:7) who acted upon a wrong principle
with disastrous results. . . . The real hours of crisis that face men
invariably occur in the commonplaces of life. . . . God's visits for
testing are always unannounced. Genesis 12:12; 14:12; 19:1.

GCM, 3:41

His choice had as its purpose, his own self-enrichment; as its
principle, compromise. "Like the garden of the Lord, like the land
of Egypt"; as its peril, that it was not a choice based on faith, but
rather the result of the process of sight and reason.

GCM, 26 Sermons, 3:45

Lot was a success to the world, "from tent to mayor's office."

GCM, 26 Sermons, p. 46

Not for the first time nor the last in human experience was it
found harder to bear prosperity than adversity. When they were
poor, uncle and nephew had no difficulty in keeping together and
sharing one fortune. But wealth divided them, introduced friction,
and ultimately forced them to separate,

Black, Listening to God, pp. 43–44

The fact is that Lot, though a pilgrim, had never really broken with
his past. It was the faith of Abraham that had moved him rather
than a faith that was his own.

GHM, Morning Sermons, p. 184

Why was it that Lot did not save Sodom? He could not help Sodom
because Sodom knew that his motive for living there was selfish,
that of gaining, getting.

GCM, 54:161

We may forget our decisions, but our decisions never forget us.

Her sons-in-law, her friends, her house, her goods, her treasure, were still in Sodom; so her heart was there also. . . . Lot's wife fled out of Sodom, led by the angel's hand, and yet she was lost. An awakened soul is not a saved soul. You are not saved till God has shut you into Christ.

M'Cheyne, *Additional Remains,* p. 256

When Abraham interceded for Sodom, he based his appeal on the righteousness of God (Gen. 18:23–33), because his nephew Lot was "a righteous man" (2 Peter 2:9). Lot may not have lived like a righteous man, but he did possess that righteousness that comes only by faith (Gen. 15:6; Rom. 4). God rescued Lot in his grace and mercy (Gen. 19:16, 19) because Lot was righteous in his sight.

Lydia (Acts 16:6–15)

A man summoned Paul to bring help to Philippi, but when Paul and his party arrived, they found a group of women at prayer, and the heart of Lydia had been prepared by God to receive the Word of the Gospel.

Is it not wonderful that the Lord can open a human heart; for he who made the lock knows well what key will fit in.

CHS, 37:489

Two women identified with Thyatira: Lydia, a businesswoman who opened her heart and her home to the Lord; and Jezebel, a false prophetess who led God's people astray (Rev. 2:18–29).

WWW

M

Mark

His mother Mary opened her house in Jerusalem to the believers for prayer (Acts 12). Mark was cousin to Barnabas (Col. 4:10) and had been led to Christ through the ministry of Peter (1 Peter 5:13). Mark had abandoned the work during Paul's first missionary journey (Acts 13:13) and Paul and Barnabas disagreed over the advisability of taking Mark along on their second journey, so Barnabas took Mark and they went their own way (Acts 15:36–41). Barnabas was concerned with what the work would do for Mark, but Paul was more concerned with what Mark would do for the work. In the end, Paul confessed that Mark was "useful" in the ministry (2 Tim. 4:11). The Lord used Mark to write the Gospel of Mark. In his association with Peter and Paul, Mark learned many important lessons in the school of faith, not the least of which was the power of prayer.

WWW

Why did Mark desert Paul and Barnabas? Was it because Paul was now the leader and Mark's cousin Barnabas was second in command (Acts 13:2, 13)? Perhaps Mark found it difficult to travel through the mountainous terrain. Was he upset because of Paul's emphasis on reaching the Gentiles? Maybe it was just plain homesickness. Whatever his reasons and mistakes, Mark proved to be a successful worker for the Lord, and he is an encouragement to anybody who has failed in serving the Lord. The victorious Christian life is a series of new beginnings, and there is always opportunity to start over again.

WWW

Martha

A woman named Martha opened her home to him [Jesus]. See Luke 10:38. When He was born, there was no room for Him in the inn (Luke 2:7). During His ministry, He had no place to lay His head (Luke 9:58).

Summarized from GCM, *The Great Physician,* p.229

Life in focus. "One thing is needful" (Luke 10:42). "One thing will I seek after" (Ps. 27:4). "One thing you are lacking" (Luke 18:22). "This one thing I do" (Phil. 3:13).

As a matter of fact, our Lord was not objecting to the "many things," but He was showing her the effect produced upon her by "many things" was that "one thing" was lacking. He was revealing to her the fact that she needed concentration at a center, and where this was so, activities could still be carried on in peace and poise and quietness.

GCM, *The Great Physician,* 229

Mary, the Mother of Our Lord

[Luke 1:46–47] Oh, you can never know the joy of Mary unless Christ becomes truly and really yours; but oh! when he is yours, yours within, reigning in your heart, yours controlling all your passions, yours changing your nature, subduing your corruptions, inspiring you with hallowed emotions; yours within, a joy unspeakable and full of glory—then you *can* sing, you *must* sing, who can restrain your tongue?

CHS, 10:719

The verb "highly favored" (Luke 1:28 KJV, NIV) is the same as "made us accepted" in Ephesians 1:6, referring to all of God's children. All true believers have been "highly graced" by the Lord.

[Luke 1:55] Covenant engagements are the softest pillows for an aching head; covenant engagements with the Surety, Jesus Christ, are the best props for a trembling spirit.

CHS, 10:723

Mary's Song (Luke 1:46–55)

The Magnificat's message is so subversive that for a period during the 1980s the government of Guatemala banned its public recitation.

Kathleen Norris, Amazing Grace, p. 117

Mary's song was humble and reverent and solidly based on Scripture. She quoted from the Song of Hannah (1 Sam. 2:1–11) as well as from the psalms. It was a joyful song, sung in the Spirit (Eph. 5:18–21). Mary had surrendered herself to the Lord to be his servant and obey his will, no matter what the cost, and her purpose was to glorify the Lord.

I should like to be able to say as long as I live, "My soul doth magnify the Lord," I should like to have this as the one motto of my life from this moment until I close my eyes in death. . . . I would fain preach that way; I would fain eat and drink that way; I would even sleep that way, so that I could truthfully say, "I have no wish but that God should be great in the eyes of others."

CHS, 51:309

Mary's last recorded words in Scripture are, "Whatever He says to you, do it" (John 2:5 NKJV). She is last found at the prayer meeting described in Acts 1:12–14.

For four rich sermons on the Magnificat (Luke 1:46–55), see *Sermons by Canon Liddon,* vol. 2 (London: Swan Sonneschein & Co., 1892), 129–88.

Mary of Bethany (Luke 10:38–42; John 11; 12:1–8)

She is mentioned three times in the Gospels, and each time, you find her at the feet of Jesus. She sat at his feet and listened to his Word; she came to his feet and wept over the death of her brother; and she brought her worship to his feet to prepare him for the cross.

A vast knowledge of the Bible will not make up for a little knowledge of the Lord.

Watchman Nee, What Shall This Man Do? p. 13

> Faithful to my Lord's commands
> I still would choose the better part,
> Serve with careful Martha's hands
> And loving Mary's heart.

Charles Wesley

The way to get the revival is to begin at the Master's feet: you must go there with Mary, and afterwards you may work with Martha.

CHS, 16:240

It is not an easy thing to maintain the balance of our spiritual life. No man can be spiritually healthy who does not meditate and commune; no man, on the other hand, is as he should be unless he is active and diligent in holy service.

CHS, 16:229

Mary had already rendered service and taken her part in the work, then sat at His feet. She left the work too soon to please Martha (Luke 10:39–40).

GCM, The Great Physician, p. 234

I do not care to over-emphasize this, but with life's experiences behind me, I am very much inclined to the conviction that the only way to enter into fellowship with His sufferings is through some suffering of our own, in which at His feet, we have discovered the sources of strength and comfort.

GCM, *The Great Physician,* p. 240

"Jesus wept" (John 11:35). . . . It is always God's attitude toward suffering. The ultimate consummation of God's love is that He will wipe away all tears from human eyes.

GCM, *The Great Physician,* p. 238

[John 12:1–11] So Mary, far from wasting, as Judas had snarled, her sentiment and substance, had heartened Jesus, and done posterity high service, and won immortal renown. The odor of her spikenard was to penetrate the world.

Carey, *Jesus and Judas,* p. 79

Note that Mary is identified with fragrance: the meal cooking in the kitchen (Luke 10:38–42), the odor of death from the tomb (John 11:32–40), the fragrance of the expensive ointment in the house (John 12).

WWW

Lord of all pots and pans and things, since I've not time to be
A saint by doing lovely things or watching late with Thee,
Or dreaming in the dawn light or storming heaven's gates,
Make me a saint by getting meals and washing up the plates.

Although I must have Martha's hands, I have a Mary mind
And when I black the boots and shoes, Thy sandals, Lord, I find.
I think of how they trod the earth, what time I scrub the floor;
Accept this meditation, Lord, I haven't time for more.

Warm all the kitchen with Thy love, and light it with Thy peace.
Forgive me all my worrying and make my grumbling cease.
Thou who didst love to give men food, in room or by the sea,
Accept this service that I do, I do it unto Thee.

Attributed to Cecily Hallack

Mary Magdalene (John 20:11–18)

And the strange thing is that, had she only known it, the cause of her grief was the joy of the ages. It was for an absent Lord that she was weeping, yet on that absence Christendom is built. . . . And so I learn that in our deepest griefs may lie the secret of our richest joys.

GHM, *The Wings of the Morning,* p. 100

A soul seeking Jesus may have Him very near and not know it.

CHS, 35:677

Melchizedek (Genesis 14:18–24)

Every one of us is met by the prince of this world and the Prince of Peace. The one tempts us with wealth, pleasure and ambition, but our Prince of Peace is ready to succor and strengthen us, in the hour of temptation.

D. L. Moody

It is not enough that Christ should be a king, for we are rebels and we need forgiveness. It is not enough that Christ should be a priest, for we are very weak and we need power. But Christ is both. He is our priest and king. He pardons and He empowers the faint. He is a priest forever, God be praised, after the order of Melchizedek.

GHM, *Morning Sermons,* 197

Moses

[Exodus 3:5] If we cannot sanctify our present situation, we will not sanctify a new one.

Moses did not go up to the mountain with a committee. If he had, he would never have come down.

Ken Blanchard

Moses was a "servant of the Lord" (Exod. 14:31; Deut. 34:5; Heb. 3:5), a title also given to Abraham (Gen. 26:24), Joshua (Josh. 24:29), David (2 Sam. 7:5), the nation of Israel (Isa. 41:8), and Jesus Christ (Isa. 42:1; 52:13).

What an honorable title! Moses is distinguished as *"the servant of Jehovah."* He was this of choice, for he willed to be the servant of God rather than to be great in the land of the Pharaohs.

CHS, 33:313

Moses was "the servant of Jehovah" and also "a man of God" (Deut. 33:1; Josh. 14:6; 1 Chron. 23:14; 2 Chron. 30:16; Ezra 3:2).

[Deuteronomy 34:5] Moses thus "died according to the word of the Lord," *for a deep dispensational reason.* It was not for Moses to give the people rest, for the law gives no man rest, and brings no man to heaven. The law may bring us to the borders of the promise, but only Joshua or Jesus can bring us into grace and truth.

CHS, 33:319

[Exodus 40:34–38] Where God's glory rests, we need not ask the way.

Watchman Nee

[Hebrews 11:24–28] There are seasons when faith shows itself in taking; there are seasons when it is witnessed in refusing.

GHM, *The Afterglow of God,* 110

The finger of God; see Exodus 31:18; Daniel 5:5; Luke 11:20; and John 8:6.

N

Nathan

General William Booth, founder of the Salvation Army, saw the prophet Nathan as a model preacher such as the Army needed.

1. Go straight to your post.
2. Give your message in the straightest possible manner.
3. Make them hear you; compel them to listen.
4. Make them understand you.
5. Don't be held back from straight dealing by any consideration for their feelings.
6. Don't be led off or hindered by any notion of the respectability of the people God sends you to warn.
7. If you have any care for yourself, you must deal straight with the people; if you do not, they will perish, and you will hear of it again.

William Booth, *Salvation Soldiery*, pp. 20–26

Nehemiah

These memoirs of Nehemiah reveal a man with the qualities of greatness. He was a man of action, resolute, practical, able to plan a great work, and with energy to carry it out. He was also a statesman, wise and prudent in the schemes he formulated, taking all the facts of the case into account. . . . And the root of every quality he possessed, the groundwork of his character, and the inspiring mainstay of his energy, was his religion, his abiding faith in the living God.

Black, According to My Gospel, p. 73

[Nehemiah 6:11] The courage which Nehemiah displayed was the courage of faith. He felt himself called to do this work, and he would do it at any cost. He believed that God was with him, and he was not going to turn tail and flee at the first sign of danger. . . . This true courage is rather steadfastness of mind, the calm, resolute fixity of purpose which holds to duty in the scorn of consequence.

Black, Listening to God, pp. 149–50

Duty cannot be maintained as an inviolate rule of life without moral courage; and courage cannot be maintained without consecration. Thus it is religion which preserves sacredness to human duty. It is the inspiring fount of noble endeavor. When a man is consumed with the desire to please God, he is long past the mere desire to please self. When the heart is fixed, the feet naturally take the path of God's commandments. The new affection moves the life to new obedience.

Black, Listening to God, p. 154

We conquer, not in any brilliant fashion—we conquer by continuing.

GHM, Highways of the Heart, p. 163

[Nehemiah 2] I like to note again that for this restoration no new material was needed. In the debris of the ruined masonry lay all the material required . . . and it seems to me that is always so when the walls of Zion are rebuilt. . . . For a revived and restored Church we want nothing that is new. What we want is a new spirit, never a new material. In the old doctrines, in the ancient truths, in the old, old story of the grace of God we have all the material that is needed for the restoration of Jerusalem.

GHM, Morning Sermons, pp. 249–50

It is deeply interesting to notice also where the citizens were put to work. Each was set to labor on the bit of wall opposite his home. . . . I do not say that men are not called to service in far distant places. . . . But I do say that for the vast majority the task that God appoints is the task lying at the door. The nearest thing is God's thing. The nearest duty is God's duty. He who cannot find his service there is little likely to be useful anywhere.

GHM, *Morning Sermons,* pp. 252–53

[Nehemiah 6:17–18] A sinful love leads to a sinful league.

Matthew Henry

[Nehemiah 8:10] Holy joy will be oil to the wheels of our obedience.

Matthew Henry

Nicodemus

Nicodemus is remembered for coming to Jesus "by night" (John 3:2; 7:50; 19:39), yet he courageously stepped out into the light and identified himself with Jesus (John 19:38–42). Note John 3:19–21.

WWW

John 3:2—"Rabbi, we know that thou art a teacher come from God"—there is a touch of flattery, and just a suggestion of patronage, in that first greeting of the Jewish doctor. He wanted a few lessons from the Master on this new kingdom which He had begun to preach. Then swiftly and sharply Jesus turns upon him: "Except a man be born again, he cannot see the kingdom." And when Nicodemus is staggered at the answer, when he gropes in the darkness not knowing what it means, Christ as it were completes his overthrow, "Art thou a master in Israel and understandest not these things?" It was severe handling, but it was infinitely kind. It arrested, penetrated, broke this Pharisee. It shattered his little code into a thousand fragments, and brought him down helpless to the feet of God.

GHM, *The Unlighted Lustre,* pp. 78–79

He came to Christ by night. It has become quite a habit to abuse him on this ground, and to say it was an act of cowardice. I do not so understand the story. . . . He came in the night for quietness and privacy. He was familiar with the messages of the past . . . but here was a new authentic Voice, and he desired to be alone with Him.

GCM, *The Great Physician,* 66

Nicodemus knew too much. That's apparent to anybody who reads the story there in the third chapter of St. John. He was an expert. His specialty was religion, and he thought he knew all there was to know about it.

Paul Scherer, *Facts That Undergird Life,* p. 3

Jesus does for Nicodemus the three things which every thorough teacher must do for every scholar. He gives him new ideas, He deepens with these ideas his personal character and responsibility, and He builds for him new relations with his fellow-man: new truth, new character, new duty.

Phillips Brooks, *The Influence of Jesus,* pp. 262–63

Noah

[Genesis 7:1] Do not shape your course and character according to the fashion of society. If you are truly born of God, you belong to a noble race which should never stoop to such degradation as that, so be righteous before the Lord. [See Ezek. 14:14, 20.]

Brooks, *The Influence of Jesus,* pp. 262–63

Notice that the Lord did not say to Noah, "Go into the ark," but "Come," plainly implying that God was himself in the ark, waiting to receive Noah and his family into the big ship that was to be their place of refuge while all the other people on the face of the earth were drowned. The distinctive word of the Gospel is a drawing word: "Come."

CHS, 56:225

Noah went in first, and his wife and children followed him. He had lived such a life as to give his children confidence in him. If you parents do not go into the ark yourselves, how can you expect your children to go in?

Moody, *Words, Work, and Workers,* pp. 144–45

Noah is the picture of one who is the Lord's witness during evil days, and lives through them faithfully, enduring unto the end.

CHS, 36:301

The original aim of Noah was to *avert* the flood.

GM-RMB, 1:99

Noah was a preacher of righteousness (2 Peter 2:5) who called people to repentance. Only the members of his family believed and were saved.

WWW

O

Obadiah (1 Kings 18)

I suspect that Elijah did not think much of Obadiah. . . . Elijah was the man of action—bold, always to the front, with nothing to conceal; Obadiah was a quiet believer, true and steadfast, but in a very difficult position, and therefore driven to perform his duty in a less open manner. His faith in the Lord swayed his life, but it did not drive him out of the court. . . . The Lord does not love that His servants, however great they are, should think lightly of their lesser comrades, and it occurs to me that he so arranged matters that Obadiah became important to Elijah when he had to face the wrathful king of Israel. The prophet is bidden to go and show himself to Ahab, and he does so; but he judges it better to begin by showing himself to the governor of his palace, that he may break the news to his master, and prepare him for the interview.

CHS, 30:553–54

God will never leave himself without a witness in this world. . . . What a horrible abode for a true believer Ahab's court must have been! If there had been no sinner there but that woman Jezebel, she was enough to make the palace a sink of iniquity. . . . Joseph feared God in the court of Pharaoh. Daniel was a trusted counselor to Nebuchadnezzar. Mordecai waited at the gate of Ahasuerus . . . and there were saints in Caesar's household.

CHS, 30:554–55

As it is horrible to find a Judas among the apostles, so it is grand
to discover an Obadiah among Ahab's courtiers.

CHS, 30:561

It is not burning quick to the death in martyrdom that is the hard
work; roasting before a slow fire is a far more terrible test of firm-
ness. To continue gracious during a long life of temptation is to
be gracious indeed.

CHS, 30:559

Onesiphorus (2 Tim. 1:16)

There were some of Paul's friends who were ashamed of his chains.
In the day of danger and adversity they forsook him. But not this
faithful friend from Ephesus. Chains are the test of friendship.
They show whether it is just a fair-weather friendship or a friendship born for adversity.

CEM, *The Woman of Tekoah,* p. 64

All the elders in Ephesus loved Paul, and had good reason to love
him, but all taken together they did not love Paul as Onesiphorus
did.

AW-BC, p. 623

Noble-hearted Onesiphorus! . . . Thou hast taught us all a much-
needed lesson tonight! For we also have friends, and especially in
the ministry, whose backs are often at the wall, whose names are
often under a cloud, and who are forsaken of all men who should
have stood by them. May we all come to be of thy vigilant and
hospitable household! May we all have thy life-long and unquench-
able loyalty to all those who suffer for righteousness' sake!

AW-BC, p. 626

P

Paul

The Man

Paul enjoyed a threefold citizenship. He was born a Jew of the tribe of Benjamin, and thus his name Saul. He was a citizen of the Roman city of Tarsus, "no mean city," and thus his name Paul. But he was primarily a citizen of heaven (Phil. 3:20–21) and devoted his life to helping others become citizens of heaven through faith in Jesus Christ.

Note the sequence of his name in the book of Acts: Saul (8:1); Barnabas and Saul (11:10; 12:25; 13:1–2, 7); Paul and his companions (13:13); Paul and Barnabas (13:42, 46, 50; 14:1).

The heart of Paul's religion is union with Christ.

James S. Stewart, *A Man in Christ,* p. 147

Christian experience does not depersonalize men and reduce them to a monotonous uniformity: it heightens every individual power they have.

Stewart, *A Man in Christ,* p. 167

Paul's religious position was hammered out, not in the study, but on the mission-field.

Stewart, *A Man in Christ,* p. 5

Let us not forget that he was a preacher first and a writer second. And both spheres—preaching and writing—were ruled by one

140

great fact—the fact of a living present Lord; and by one all-decisive
experience—the experience of union and communion with Him.

Stewart, *A Man in Christ,* p. 8

What meets us in his epistles is not a man creating a new religion,
or even giving a new direction to one already existing: it is simply
the Gospel of Jesus in action, the original, authentic Gospel first
changing a man's life, and thereafter molding all his thought.

Stewart, *A Man in Christ,* p. 19

He was at once a Jew, and a citizen of the wider world. . . . Jewish lineage, he felt, was not a thing to be apologetic about: on the
contrary, it was a unique cause for thanksgiving.

Stewart, *A Man in Christ,* pp. 32–33

Wandering [Stoic] scholars and orators carried the message far and
wide. It was the day of itinerant preachers . . . and in the streets
and marketplaces of Asia Minor and Europe the Stoic evangelist
was a familiar figure. . . . It is no wonder that, in that weary, disil-
lusioned world, men stopped to listen.

Stewart, *A Man in Christ,* p. 57

His converts were his pride and joy. When he writes to them he
is like a father addressing his children. He commends everything
that is praiseworthy in them, where others might have found little
enough to commend. He scolds them for their shortcomings, and
warns them that if they do not mend their ways he will take a big
stick with him next time he comes (1 Cor. 4:21). But he encourages
them for all he is worth, and makes no secret of his consuming
desire that they should grow up to be hundred-per-cent Christians,
worthy of the honorable name they bear.

F. F. Bruce, *Paul: Apostle of the Heart Set Free,* p. 459

Four themes emphasized in his teaching call for summary mention because they still need to be emphasized. (a) True religion is
not a matter of rules and regulations. . . . (b) In Christ men and
women have come of age, as the new humanity brought into being
through his death and resurrection-life. . . . (c) People matter more

than things, more than principles, more than causes. The highest of principles and the best of causes exist for the sake of people; to sacrifice people to them is a perversion of the true order. (d) Unfair discrimination on the grounds of race, religion, class or sex is an offense against God and humanity alike.

Bruce, Paul, p. 463

Take away the cross of Christ from Paul, and he is as weak as any other man.

AW-BC, p. 655

The apostle Paul had one of those arresting magnetic personalities that inevitably produces a polarizing effect upon those around them. When confronted with his dynamic, disciplined, decisive character, they were compelled to react.

D. Edmund Hiebert, Personalities Around Paul, p. 13

His Conversion (Acts 9, 22, 26)

Note that the description of the light that Paul saw becomes more vivid: "a light" (9:3); "a great light from heaven" (22:6); "a light from heaven . . . brighter than the sun" (26:13). See Proverbs 4:18.

WWW

Paul wrote that his conversion was "a pattern" to those who would believe afterwards (1 Tim. 1:16). He saw the light, heard the voice, fell down in fear before God, and trusted the Savior. At the return of Jesus Christ, the people of Israel will have a similar experience of sudden conversion (Zech. 12:10–13:1), and Paul considered himself "born out of due time" (1 Cor. 15:8). God's longsuffering and mercy proved to Paul that he would so deal with other sinners who, unlike him, were not the "chief of sinners."

That long-suffering was seen first in *sparing his life* when he was rushing headlong in sin, breathing out threatening, foaming at the mouth with denunciations of the Nazarene and his people. If the Lord had but lifted his finger, Saul would have

been crushed like a moth, but almighty wrath forbore, and the
rebel lived on.

CHS, 59:392

The first time we see Saul of Tarsus he is silently consenting to
Stephen's death. . . . But, beginning with his silent consent to the
death of Stephen, Saul soon went on to plan and to perpetuate
the most dreadful deeds on his own account.

AW-BC, p. 640

The apostle's language in the text, "for a pattern," may mean that
he was what printers call a first proof, an early impression from
the engraving, a specimen of those to follow.

CHS, 59:385

[Acts 9:11] Poor Saul had been led to cry for mercy, and the moment he began to pray God began to hear. Do you not notice, in
reading the chapter, what attention God paid to Saul? He knew
the street where he lived: "Go to the street that is called Straight."
He knew the house where he resided: "Enquire at the house of
Judas." He knew his name; it was *Saul*. He knew the place where
he came from: "Enquire for Saul of *Tarsus*." And he knew that he
had prayed: "Behold, *he prayeth*."

CHS, 1:118

In every case the individual is saved, not for himself alone, but
with a view to the good of others. . . . *Paul's conversion had an im-
mediate relation to the conversion of many others.*

CHS, 59:386–87

Paul in Arabia (Gal. 1:17)

But, somehow, Sinai seems to have drawn Paul to the awful solitudes with an irresistible attraction and strength. It may have been
an old desire of his formed at Gamaliel's feet, some day to see the
Mount of God with his own eyes. He may have said to himself that
he must hide himself for once in that cleft-rock before he sat down

to his life-work in Moses' seat. "I must see Rome," he said towards the end of his life. "I must see Sinai," he also said, at the beginning of his life. . . . [J]udge him not by his outward appearance. For he carries Augustine, and Luther, and Calvin and Knox, in his fruitful loins. In that lonely stranger you are now looking at, and in his seed, shall all the families of the earth be blessed. . . . Never did any other lord receive his own again with such usury as when Paul went into Arabia with Moses and the Prophets and the Psalms in his knapsack, and returned to Damascus with the Romans and the Ephesians and the Colossians in his mouth and in his heart.

AW-BC, p. 646

But the Apostle's chief reason for telling us about Arabia at all is this, to prove to us, and to impress upon us, that it was not cities and colleges and books that made him what by that time he was made. It was God Himself who made Paul the Apostle he was made. "I conferred not with flesh and blood," he protests.

AW-BC, p. 649

His Thorn in the Flesh (2 Corinthians 12)

There was a colossal pride in Paul, and at the same time a prostrate humility, such that they had never seen anything like it in any other man; a submissiveness and a self-surrender to all men.

AW-BC, p. 660

Paul's Master had taken the proper precautions at the beginning of Paul's apostleship that he should be all through it, and down to the end of it, the humblest man in all the world. By that terrible thorn in his flesh; by a conscience full of the most remorseful memories; as well as by incessant trials and persecutions and sufferings of all conceivable kinds, Paul was made and was kept the humblest of all humble men.

AW-BC, p. 662

We are plainly taught how mistaken we are when we set the eminent saints of the olden times upon a platform by themselves, as though they were a class of super-human beings. . . . They fought the common fight, and won by strength available to all believers; let us esteem them as our brethren, and with them pursue the sacred conflict in the name of the common leader. [L]et us run as they ran, that we may win as they won, and may glorify God in our day and generation, as they did in theirs.

CHS, 18:674

He reckoned his great trial to be a gift. It is well put. He does not say, "There was inflicted upon me a thorn in the flesh" but "There was given to me." This is holy reckoning.

CHS, 18:678

From all this I gather, that the worst trial a man may have may be the best possession he has in this world; that the messenger of Satan may be as good to him as his guardian angel; that it may be as well for him to be buffeted of Satan as ever it was to be caressed by the Lord himself; that it may be essential to our soul's salvation that we should do business not only in deep waters, but on waters that cast up mire and dirt. The worst form of trial may, nevertheless, be our best present portion.

CHS, 18:681

Without the sanctifying power of the Holy Spirit, thorns are productive of evil rather than good. In many people, their thorn in the flesh does not appear to have fulfilled any admirable design at all; it has created another vice, instead of removing a temptation.

CHS, 18:683

If the thorn be a blessing, what must the blessing itself be? If the smarts of earth heal us, what will the joys of heaven do for us? Let us be glad! Ours is a happy portion!

CHS, 18:684

[2 Corinthians 12:9] The Greek word translated "rest" (KJV) means "to overshadow, to tabernacle" (John 1:14; Rev. 7:15). Paul was suffering, yet he saw himself as the Old Testament Jews saw the tabernacle: indwelt and overshadowed by the glory of God. Like that of the tabernacle, his outward appearance was common and weak, but within he was a holy of holies that radiated the glory of God. See 2 Corinthians 4:7–5:8.

Paul had experienced a remarkable blessing when he was caught up into the third heaven, but God had to balance that glory with suffering. However, the suffering plus the grace of God helped to produce in Paul a new glory—victory over the temptation to pride. Great blessings can present great temptations, and we must be on our guard.

WWW

[W]e should never know how sufficient grace was if it were not for these troubles.

CHS, 52:79

Paul in Prison

2 Tim. 4:13—He is inspired, and yet he wants books! He has been preaching for at least thirty years, and yet he wants books! He has seen the Lord, and yet he wants books! He had had a wider experience than most men, and yet he wants books! He had been caught up into the third heaven, and had heard things which it was unlawful for a man to utter, yet he wants books! He had written the major part of the New Testament, and yet he wants books! The apostle says to Timothy and so he says to every preacher, "Give thyself unto reading."

CHS, 9:668

[2 Timothy] Now, how shall we find the old man? What sort of temper will he be in? We find him *full of confidence in the religion which has cost him so much* (1:12). . . . You will notice that this grand old man is *having communion with Jesus Christ in his suffer-ings* (2:10). . . . Not only is he confident for the past, and in sweet communion for the present, but *he is resigned for the future* (4:6). . . . [W]e find him not only resigned but *triumphant* (4:7). . . . Once more; he not only triumphs in the present, but he *is in expectation*

*of a crown (4:8). . . . [E]verything which the apostle thought of was
connected with Christ.*

CHS, 9:669–72

Peter

The Man

He was genuinely human. That is good. Whenever a minister becomes more minister than man, three strikes have been called on him. Peter was always himself. He never struck a pose. He never pretended. He never tried to hide his ignorance. Peter had gifts of leadership. He had that something that we call personality. A third quality we like about Peter is his wholeheartedness. He was sometimes on the wrong side of the fence, sometimes on the right side. But he never straddled it.

Clovis Chappell, Sermons on Simon Peter, pp. 10–11

Peter was a man of too great self-confidence. . . . He was also an exceedingly impulsive man. He reasoned with his feelings rather than with his mind. . . . Living within the realm of his emotions, Peter was unpredictable and unreliable. . . . He [Jesus] gave Simon a glimpse of his possibilities. Our Lord, seeing Simon for what he was, saw also what he might become. . . . To each he is saying, "You are; you shall be."

Chappell, Sermons on Simon Peter, pp. 10–15

I have known many a poor sinner pluck up hope as he has observed the sins and struggles of those who were saved by grace, and I have known many of the heirs of heaven find consolation as they have observed how imperfect beings have prevailed with God in prayer, and have been delivered in their time of distress. I am very glad that the apostles were not perfect men; they would then have understood all that Jesus said at once, and we should have lost our Lord's instructive explanations; they would also have lived above all trouble of mind, and then the Master would not have said to them these golden words, "Let not your heart be troubled."

CHS, 29:517

"Thou art Simon the son of Jona; thou shalt be called Cephas, which is by interpretation, A stone" (John 1:42). . . . Jona means a dove, and Cephas and Peter mean a rock. So what Jesus is saying to Peter is: "Up until now you have been like a fluttering, timorous dove; but if you take me as Master, and if you give your life to me, I will make you a rock."

Barclay, The Master's Men, p. 16

Mark's gospel is nothing other than the preaching material of Peter. It must always stand to the honor of Peter that he kept nothing back. He tells of his own mistakes, of the rebukes he sometimes received from his Master, of his own terrible disloyalty. Peter concealed nothing, for he wished to show the lengths to which the forgiving love and the re-creating grace of Christ had gone for him.

Barclay, The Master's Men, p. 17

For some queer reason, we seem to love people more when they are not too perfect. In the presence of a faultless saint, the average one of us feels ill at ease. . . . This may be the reason Christians have always felt a special affection for Simon Peter. . . . Peter contained or has been associated with more contradictions than almost any other Bible character. He appeared to be a combination of courage and cowardice, reverence and disrespect, selfless devotion and dangerous self-love. . . . Anyway, we are glad Peter lived, and we are glad Christ found him. He is so much like so many of us, at least in his weaknesses. It only remains for us to learn the secret of his strength.

A. W. Tozer, We Travel an Appointed Way, pp. 103–6

He was a man of intellectual capacity, as is seen quite simply in the fact that the records speak of him as asking more questions than any of the disciples. . . . That he was a man full of human emotion needs no argument. . . . Moreover, he was a man of tremendous willpower. . . . Thus all the elements of great personality were found in Simon, and yet he was a weak man. He lacked an element welding the elemental things into consistency and strength. . . . Every jewel is a combination of elements welded into strength.

GCM, The Great Physician, pp. 34–35

Without Jesus, Peter might have been a good fisherman, perhaps even a very good one. But he would never have gotten anywhere, would never have learned what a coward he really was, what a confused, then confessing, courageous person he was, even a good preacher (Acts 2) when he needed to be. Peter stands out as a true individual, or better, a true character, not because he had become "free" or "his own person," but because he had become attached to the Messiah and messianic community, which enabled him to lay hold of his life, to make so much more of his life than if he had been left to his own devices.

Stanley Hauerwas and William H. Willimon, Resident Aliens, p. 65

When Simon Peter first steps upon the scene he is a rash, impulsive, and impetuous man. One recognizes the slumbering greatness of him; but one feels the boundless possibilities of evil. But Jesus handles him and plays upon him as a master musician might play on his loved instrument, till the chords are wakened into such glorious music that the centuries are ringing with it still.

GHM, Sunrise: Addresses from a City Pulpit, p. 88

He left his boats and his nets and his fish, and he gained the friendship of Christ, which was worth more than all the world.

Moody, Words, Work, and Workers, p. 242

Watchman Nee reminds us that the New Testament records three occasions on which Peter was interrupted: on the Mount of Transfiguration by God the Father (Matt. 17:4–5); in Capernaum by God the Son (Matt. 17:25); and in the home of Cornelius by God the Holy Spirit (Acts 10:44). See chapter 2 of his book *What Shall This Man Do?*

G. Campbell Morgan points out that three times Jesus took Peter, James, and John alone with him: to the Mount of Transfiguration (Matt. 17:1); into the home of Jairus (Luke 8:51); and into the Garden of Gethsemane (Mark 14:32–33). In each experience, he taught them something about death: he was glorified in death, he was victorious over death, and he was submissive to the Father's will in death. See pages 246–50 of his book *The Crises of the Christ*. Note the parallel between these three events and Philippians 3:10.

In the Gospels and Acts, at least twelve miracles are recorded that relate directly to Peter. For an exposition of these miracles, see my book *Your Next Miracle*.

His Confession of Faith

[Matthew 16:17, 23] "Blessed art thou, Simon Bar-jonah. . . . Get thee behind me, Satan. . . ." The first saying marks the moment when He first heard from human lips the confession He had long craved to hear. The second saying discloses Jesus facing again the besetting temptation of His life. . . . He saw Satan transfigured into an angel of light. . . . We find with a shock of surprise that the man who is exalted to heaven in one saying is cast down to hell in another. . . . A man may awake in the morning with a psalm, and before the sun has set make his bed in hell. [There is a need] for *a vigilant watchfulness over the life.* "Let him that thinketh he standeth take heed lest he fall."

William M. Clow, *The Secret of the Lord,* pp. 83–95

"The gates of Hades shall not prevail against it." The figure employed suggests not defensive strength, but aggressive strength. A simple consideration of the figure of speech shows that it cannot mean defense, because no attacking city carries its gates with it. The Church is rather seen at war, and the declaration is made that the gates of Hades shall not prevail against it. . . . The figure is really that of escape from Hades. The Church is seen opening up a way of escape from a beleaguered city. Here the Lord, surveying the whole field of the conflict, refers to the last enemy which is to be destroyed, which is death, and declares that that must yield to the onward march of His soldiers. The great enemies of the human race are sin, sorrow, and death, and in that order. [The] Lord saw His Church as an aggressive force conquering sin, overcoming sorrow, and therefore triumphant over death.

GCM, *Peter and the Church,* pp. 20–21

Walking on the Water (Matt. 14:22–33)

In Luke 5:1–11, Peter learned he could trust Jesus to do miracles
in the daytime on calm water, and in Mark 4:35–41 that he could
trust Jesus in the nighttime in stormy weather, even when the Lord
was asleep. But the Matthew 14 experience taught Peter that he
could trust Jesus when the Master was not in the boat *and when
Peter was not in the boat!* Our Lord used several "sea miracles" to
teach Peter some valuable lessons.

WWW

This is the story of one of the most wonderful pre-Pentecostal
experiences of Peter. While it reveals an element of failure,
that is not its only quality, neither is it its chief one. That element of failure, however, has so impressed us that we are in
danger of failing to observe that it was failure on a singularly
high level, failure in an hour of exalted and Christ-honoring
experience. While we must not ignore the failure, we ought to
consider it in the light of the whole story, for it is a story full
of bright and tender light. . . . Briefly: an exalted experience,
a sudden defeat, a fulfilled purpose.

GCM, 7:34–35

It is the story of a man who, suddenly lifted to a wonderful height,
saw the possibility of the impossible in fellowship with Christ;
asked for permission, waited for orders, and, having received
them, obeyed and actually walked on the waters just as his Lord
had been walking on the waters.

GCM, 7:39

[Matthew 14:30] There are two sights in human life which fill the
heart with profound sorrow. The first is that of the person who
has sunk. . . . But to the seeing eye and the perceiving heart there
is another spectacle which is not less tragical—and that is of the
man who is *beginning to sink.* . . . Our perils do not always reach
us through our worst. Our perils sometimes reach us through
our best; through what is charming in us, and delightful, and
self-forgetful, and enthusiastic. . . . Peter began to sink *in very*

familiar waters. . . . Also to be noted is this fact, that Peter began to sink *on a permitted path.* . . . Equally notable is this, too, that Peter began to sink *when he began to fear.* . . . [W]hen Peter began to sink, *his Saviour was not far away.*

Summarized from GHM, *The Wind on the Heath,* pp. 41–51

The wise man in the storm prays God, not for safety from danger, but for deliverance from fear. It is the storm within which endangers him, not the storm without.

Ralph Waldo Emerson

[M]y first observation upon it is that it was a very brief prayer. There were only three words in it: "Lord, save me." I believe that the excellence of prayer often consists in its brevity. . . . I would urge you to cultivate the habit of praying briefly all the day.

CHS, 56:99–100

It was a short prayer and right to the point: "Lord, save me." It didn't begin with a long preamble, as a great many prayers do. If it had taken him as long to come to what he wanted to say as it does some people in our prayer meetings, he would have been forty feet under water before he would have reached it.

Moody, *Words, Work, and Workers,* p. 243

The apostles were in a storm, not because, like Jonah, they disobeyed the Lord but because they obeyed him. It was more dangerous for the apostles to remain with the crowd that wanted to make Jesus king (John 6:15ff) than to launch out on the sea.

His Denial of Christ

The great lesson of Peter's denial is that wherever there is arrested development of Christian life there must follow deterioration of Christian character. Life must make progress to higher levels or sink lower until it pass away.

GCM, 1:193

[The stages leading to Peter's denial of Christ.] First, refusal to follow his Lord into the mystery of pain and refusal to believe that his Lord knew best. Next, boastfulness. "Although all shall be offended, yet will not I." What follows? Failure in the devotional life, inability to watch, and the cessation of prayer. Then zeal without knowledge, hastiness, the drawing of a sword, not under the command of his Master.

GCM, 1:194

That Peter followed "afar off" was not his sin; it was that he followed at all. "Let these go their way," said Jesus, a signal for the apostles to get out of the garden. "I will smite the shepherd and the sheep will be scattered." By following, Peter walked into temptation and shameful failure. Note that the sequence parallels Psalm 1:1. Peter rejected Christ's counsel ("Let these go their way") and walked in the counsel of the ungodly (Luke 22:54; John 18:15). Then he stood "in the way of sinners" (John 18:16–18), and finally sat down "in the seat of the scornful" (Luke 22:55). On a night when Jesus was sweating as it were "great drops of blood," Peter was warming himself at the enemy's fire.

WWW

The Church of God today is cursed by zeal without knowledge. This is the age of fussy feverishness, and there are multitudes of people who are attempting to overtake their lack of spiritual life by service. . . . It is well for us to remember that the last act of Divine surgery which the hand of Jesus ever performed was made necessary by the blundering zeal of a distant disciple.

GCM, 1:198–99

George Morrison called Peter's attack on Malchus "impulsive loyalty."

GHM, *Wind on the Heath,* p. 261

Peter's fall . . . is four times recorded, at considerable length; but it is not once excused. . . . It was a very sad fall because it was *the fall of one of the most favored of Christ's disciples.* . . . Peter's fall was especially sad because *he had been faithfully warned concerning it.* . . . Further, the guilt of Peter's sin is enhanced by the fact that *it came so soon after his protestation of fidelity to his Master.*

CHS, 48:133

His Restoration

Peter was helped by the ministry of memory (Luke 22:61). . . .
Yet let us bear in mind that while such use of memory is good,
it is only a second best. Had Peter used his memory as the Lord
had purposed, it would have served as a preventive rather than
as only a cure. . . . Peter was helped toward recovery by a look.
"And the Lord turned and looked at Peter" (Luke 22:61). What do
you suppose Peter read in the face of Jesus? He read no anger, no
contempt, no bitter resentment. He read no self-pity, no despair.
But he did read heartache, grief and sorrow beyond words. He read
also a deathless yearning. He read an incredible love that simply
refused to let him go. . . . "He went out and wept bitterly." This,
I take it, marks the final step in Peter's recovery.

Chappell, Sermons on Simon Peter, pp. 44–47

But there was one thing . . . which we must never forget; that
is, *the prayer of Christ for Peter*. He said to him, "I have prayed
for thee," and the effect of that prayer was made apparent in the
apostle's restoration.

CHS, 48:139

Even when Peter went out and wept bitterly, there was a song singing itself over and over in the depths of his stricken soul. *"When
thou art converted . . . strengthen thy brethren."* What did it mean?
It meant that his Master had foreseen the fall with all its baseness
and its treachery—*"thou shalt deny Me thrice."* But it meant also
that his Master, knowing the very, very worst, had yet confidently
anticipated the dawning of a day in which the coward should be
the bravest of the brave and in which the weakling should be the
fortifier of all the apostolic band. It was by means of a sublime
expectation that Peter was led from the depths of shame to a life
of service and a martyr's crown.

F. W. Boreham, Shadows on the Wall, p. 22

He has gone astray, and he has been brought back; what better
can he do than to strengthen his brethren? *He will thus help to undo*

the evil which he has wrought. . . . Besides, *how can you better express your gratitude to God . . . ?*

CHS, 34:413–14

He can strengthen them by telling them of *the bitterness of denying his Master.* Again, Peter was the man to tell another of *the weakness of the flesh. . . .* And could not Peter speak about *the love of Jesus to poor wanderers? . . .* And could not Peter fully describe *the joy of restoration?*

CHS, 34:416–17

His Vision (Acts 10)

Peter had been given the keys of the kingdom of heaven, not the keys of heaven, where the gates are never shut. By sharing the Gospel, he opened the door of faith to the Jews at Pentecost (Acts 2) and then to the Samaritans (Acts 8:1–25). By this vision, God was preparing him to take the message to the Gentiles.

[Acts 10:14] "Not so, Lord." This is a very curious expression. . . . If Peter had said, "Not so," there would have been a clear consistency in his language and tone. But "Not so, *Lord,*" is an off jumble of self-will and reverence, of pride and humility, of contradiction and devotion. Surely, when you say "Not so," it ought not to be said to the Lord; and if you say "Lord," you ought not to put side by side with such an ascription the expression, "Not so."

CHS, 31:85

But Peter is Peter still, and so does the renewed man betray the infirmities which were with him before his renewal.

CHS, 31:89

Delivered from Prison (Acts 12)

Three powers are revealed in this event: the power of a corrupt leader, the power of a praying church, and the power of a godly servant. Satan attacked Peter because Peter's ministry was attacking Satan's strongholds. Satan knew Peter and Paul (Acts 19:15) and opposed them. In Acts 12, Satan came as a lion to devour; in Acts 19, he came as a serpent to deceive.

WWW

The angel fetched Peter out of prison, but it was prayer that fetched the angel.

Thomas Watson

[Acts 12:16] It is perilous to judge a person by one action. Life is too complex and intricate for that. . . . There was an hour, for instance, when Peter drew his sword and cut off the ear of the priest's servant. There was another hour . . . when, panic-stricken, he denied his Lord. But if I wished to know the real Peter I should not turn to either of these hours; I should rather choose an action such as this—*Peter continued knocking.* Shall I tell you what it reveals in the apostle? . . . In the first place, this common act shows Peter's *courage.* . . . The truest courage in this life of ours is seldom momentary or spectacular. It moves in the shadow of the dreary street; dwells in the dull seclusion of the home; continues doing things, with quiet heart, when the natural impulse would be to turn and flee. . . . [T]his common action reveals to us Peter's *understanding.* . . . Half an hour earlier Peter had seen an angel, and he had been dazed and thought it was a [vision]; and now *they* think that Peter is a ghost, and Peter instantly grasps the situation. . . . Then, in the third place, this common action reveals to us Peter's *consecration.* . . . Peter had had an experience that morning which had lifted him up into the courts of heaven. . . . A little while before . . . Peter had come to a great iron gate. And at a single touch of the angelic finger that gate had opened to let Peter through. And now he was at no massive iron gate, but at the humble door of a very humble dwelling—and he continued knocking.

GHM, *Wind on the Heath,* pp. 90–96

Pontius Pilate

Pilate is mentioned fifty-five times in the Greek text of the New Testament: fifty-one times in the Gospels, three times in Acts (3:13; 4:27;

13:28), and once in the epistles (1 Tim. 6:13 NIV). Yet he is mentioned each Lord's Day in thousands of churches when God's people
recite the Apostles' Creed—"Suffered under Pontius Pilate."

It was Pontius Pilate who crucified our Lord. But for Pontius Pilate
our Lord would not have been crucified. In spite of Pontius Pilate
our Lord might have been stoned to death before the palace of
the high priest that passover morning. Or, lest there should be an
uproar among the people, He might have been fallen upon and
murdered when He was on His knees in the Garden of Gethsemane
that passover night.

AW-BC, p. 513

Note Pilate's fear and indecision as recorded in John 18–19. He
spoke to Jesus and then went out to the people (18:29), went back
in (18:33), and then went out again (18:38). He went back into his
judgment hall and allowed the soldiers to abuse Jesus, and then
he went out with Jesus (19:1–7). He returned to the judgment
hall with Jesus (19:9) and heard the people shouting against him
(19:12). He went out for the fourth time (19:13) and finally capitu-
lated to the crowd. He kept having second thoughts, and second
thoughts usually lead people to make the wrong decision.

WWW

How are we to reach Pilate? How are we to give him warning?
He has rejected the voice of Jesus and the sight of Jesus—could
not Peter be fetched to expostulate with him? Alas, he has denied
his Master. Could not John be brought in? Even he has forsaken
the Lord. Where shall a messenger be found? It shall be found
in a dream. God can get at men's hearts, however hardened they
may be. Never give them up, never despair of arousing them. If
my ministry, your ministry, and the ministry of the blessed Book
should all seem to be nothing, God can reach the conscience by
a dream.

CHS, 28:127

Of all persons in Jerusalem at the time of the trial of Jesus, whether
Jew or Gentile, friend or foe, disciple or stranger, this woman, the

wife of Pilate, is the only one who dares to say a word on behalf of the lonely prisoner.

CEM, The Way of a Man with a Maid, p. 136

With all his heart would Pilate have fallen in with his wife's warning, had it been possible for him to do so. He did not need her urgent message. He knew far better than she did that the prisoner at his bar was a just man, and something more than a just man, but that only tied up Pilate's hands all the tighter. "Have thou nothing to do with that just man!" Yes; but how is Pilate to get rid of that just man? . . . You all know what he did next. He put up Jesus to the vote of the people against Barabbas, trusting that the gratitude and the pity and the sense of fairplay among the common people would carry the day.

AW-BC, pp. 516–18

["What is truth?" John 18:38] The lesson which we are to draw from this verse must depend upon the view we take of the spirit in which the words were spoken. Some of the best commentators conceive them to have been words of mockery; and such is the great Lord Bacon's view. "'What is truth?' said jesting Pilate, and would not wait for a reply."

In all deference to such authority, we cannot believe that this sentence was spoken in jest. In Pilate's whole conduct there is no trace of such a tone. It betrays throughout much of uncertainty, nothing of lightness. He was cruelly tormented with the perplexity of efforts to save his prisoner. He risked his own reputation. He pronounced Him, almost with vehemence, to be innocent. He even felt awe, and was afraid of Him. . . . Out of that mood, when he heard the enthusiast before him speak of a Kingdom of the Truth, there broke a sad, bitter, sarcastic sigh, "What is Truth?"

F. W. Robertson, Sermons, 1:292–93

To such a character Jesus would not explain His Truth. He gave no reply: He held His peace. God's Truth is too sacred to be expounded to superficial worldliness in its transient fit of earnestness.

F. W. Robertson, Sermons, 1:297

Now—the appointed ways to teach this Truth. They are three: Independence—Humbleness—Action. [Independence means] a determination to trust in God rather than in man to teach, in God and God's light in the soul. Second, Humbleness. There is no infallibility in man. . . . We may err: that one thought is enough to keep a man humble. . . . Lastly, Action. This was Christ's rule—"If any man will *do* His will. . . ." God says, Act—make the life true, and then you will be able to believe. Live in earnest, and you will know the answer to "What is Truth?"

F. W. Robertson, *Sermons,* 1:301–3

Pilate treats the whole matter cavalierly; he is a proud and haughty Roman; he hates the people whom he governs, and though he has a conscience, and at the first he shows a tenderness towards his prisoner, yet his chief end and aim was to keep his office and amass money, and therefore innocent blood must be spilt.

CHS, 28:95

"Jesus gave him no answer." And a large portion of the inquisitive questioning to which we have to submit is not worth answering; nor is it worthwhile for you and me to go up and down the world fishing for questions, or inviting the objections and cavillings of skeptics, because we think ourselves so exceedingly clever that we are easily able to answer them. . . . Our Saviour invited no questions from Pilate; he did not even condescend to answer all that Pilate had to say to him; and the best thing for a Christian to do, in many of his times of trial, is to say, with David, "I was dumb with silence. I held my peace, even from good; and my sorrow was stirred."

CHS, 49:169–70

Our Lord, in effect, tells us that truth is the pre-eminent characteristic of his kingdom, and that his royal power over men's hearts is through the truth. . . . He dealt not with fiction, but with facts; not with trifles, but with infinite realities. . . . Our Lord's testimony was pre-eminently practical and matter-of-fact, full of verities and certainties. . . . What concern have dying men with the thousand trivial questions which are flitting around us?

CHS, 18:702–3

Christ never came to set up his kingdom by force of arms. . . . Christ said to Peter, "Put up thy sword into its sheath." No compulsion ought to be used with any man to lead him to receive any opinion, much less to induce him to espouse the truth. Falsehood requires the rack of the Inquisition, but truth needs not such unworthy aid; her own beauty, and the Spirit of God, are her strength. . . . Believe me, no kingdom is worthy of the Lord Jesus but that which has its foundations laid in indisputable verities; Jesus would scorn to reign by the help of a lie.

CHS, 18:704–5

The battle is over, and Pilate had lost. Satan had won. Pilate called for a basin of water and, washing his hands in it before the multitude, said, "I am innocent of the blood of this just person: see ye to it." . . . What a drama that was—Pilate struggling for his soul; his reason, his judgment, his fears, his superstition all urging him to do the right; yet over all these obstacles and warning he marched on to his great crime and henceforth will be known forever as that "Pontius Pilate under whom Jesus suffered."

CEM, *Great Interviews of Jesus,* pp. 145–46

"What then shall I do with Jesus who is called Christ?" That is your question and mine as well as that of Pilate. It is intensely personal for us. We cannot shirk it. We cannot remain neutral. We can no more remain neutral toward Christ than we can remain neutral toward the multiplication table. We can no more remain neutral toward him than we can remain neutral to the law of gravitation or to the law of sowing and reaping. Every man of us has Christ on our hands. We must decide for him or we must decide against him. God pity us when we try to pass that responsibility to anyone else!

Clovis Chappell, *Faces About the Cross,* p. 120

Q

Quartus, "A Brother" (Romans 16:23)

The *Dictionary of Paul and His Letters* (IVP) contains an excellent article by E. E. Ellis on "Paul and His Coworkers" in which he names thirty-six people who were associated with Paul in his ministry. Of course, there were many unnamed believers who worked alongside Paul, but even some who are named are a mystery to us, and one of them is "our brother Quartus" (Rom. 16:23). His name is last on a list of eight believers in Corinth who sent greetings to the saints in Rome (Rom. 16:21–23). Quartus did not have the stature of Timothy or the secretarial ability of Tertius, to whom Paul dictated the letter, nor did he hold any prominent civic office like Erastus. But he was a member of the family of God and wanted to send his love to Paul's friends (16:1–16) and to all the saints who would hear the epistle read to the congregations in Rome.

In his sermon "Quartus, A Brother" (*Week-Day Evening Addresses*), Alexander Maclaren brings out some practical truths that should be considered by believers today:

He is only a good, simple, unknown Christian. He feels a spring of love open in his heart to these brethren far across the sea, whom he never met. He would like them to know that he thought lovingly of them, and to be lovingly thought of by them. So he begs a little corner in Paul's letter, and gets it. . . . The first thing that strikes me in connection with these words is, how deep and real they show that new bond of Christian love to have been.

p. 125

It is impossible for us to throw ourselves completely back to the condition of things which the Gospel found. . . . Great gulfs of national hatred, of fierce enmities of race, language and religion; wide separations of social conditions, far profounder than anything of the sort which we know, split mankind into fragments. On the one side was the freeman, on the other, the slave; on the one side, the Gentile, on the other, the Jew; on the one side, the insolence and hard-handedness of Roman rule, on the other, the impotent, and, therefore, envenomed hatred of conquered peoples. . . . Into this hideous condition of things the Gospel comes, and silently flings its clasping tendrils over the wide gaps, and binds the crumbling structure of human society with a new bond, real and living. . . . "There is neither Jew nor Greek, there is neither bond nor free, there is neither male nor female, for ye are all one in Christ Jesus" (Gal. 3:28).

pp. 126, 128

As if he had said, "Never mind telling them anything about what I am, what place I hold, or what I do. Tell them I am a brother, that will be enough. It is the only name by which I care to be known; it is the name which explains my love to them."

p. 129

Another remark is, how strangely and unwittingly this good man has got himself an immortality by that passing thought of his. One loving message has won for him the prize for which men have joyfully given life itself—an eternal place in history. Wherever the Gospel is preached there also shall this be told as a memorial of him. . . . And how much ashamed some of the other people in the New Testament would have been if they had known that their passing faults—the quarrel of Euodia and Syntyche for instance—were to be gibbetted forever in the same fashion! . . . Let us live so that each act if recorded would shine with some modest ray of true light like brother Quartus' greeting.

pp. 130–31

Queen of Sheba (1 Kings 10:1–13)

The first thing that is told us concerning the Queen of Sheba is this, that she had heard in Sheba concerning the Name of the Lord. . . . For the Name of the Lord is "The Lord God, merciful and gracious, longsuffering, and abundant in goodness and truth, keeping mercy for thousands, forgiving iniquity and transgression and sin." . . . The Queen of Sheba had lords many and gods many of her own. . . . But there was no name of any god given in Sheba that took such hold of the Queen of Sheba's heart as did the Name of the Lord God of Israel.

                                                    AW-BC, pp. 292–93

Alexander Whyte imagines the Queen of Sheba riding back to her land and carrying a copy of the prayer Solomon prayed at the dedication of the temple, especially 1 Kings 8:42–43. This is the promise to "foreigners" that Jehovah would hear their prayers if they prayed toward the temple. He suggests that the queen was truly converted to faith in the God of Israel (pp. 296–97). Centuries later, another Ethiopian, a high official, was riding home in his chariot, reading the prophet Isaiah, and Philip the evangelist led him to faith in Christ (Acts 8:26–40).

Jesus pointed to the Queen of Sheba as a witness against the generation of Israelites in his day, for she traveled a long way to hear the wisdom of Solomon, and here was the Son of God—a "greater than Solomon"—in their very midst (Matt. 12:42). Jesus is greater than Solomon, for he is the very Son of God and the King of Kings. He is greater in wealth and wisdom (Col. 2:3), and he is building a greater temple than Solomon built (Eph. 2:19–22).

                                                            WWW

R

Rahab (Joshua 2; 6:23)

Because of her faith, Rahab was part of the ancestry of the Lord Jesus Christ (Matt. 1:5), was named in the faith "Hall of Fame" (Heb. 11:31), and was used by James as an example of faith leading to good works (James 2:25). Her spiritual experience was like that of the believers in Thessalonica (1 Thess. 1:9).

Moses had sent twelve spies into Canaan and only two of them, Caleb and Joshua, had faith to believe God could give Israel the land (Num. 13). Perhaps that is why Joshua sent only two spies into Canaan!

Rahab's faith possessed her entire personality. She had fear because she heard how Israel's God had delivered the Jews from Egypt and destroyed the Gentile nations. She knew enough facts about God to want to trust him. "I know that the LORD has given you the land" (Josh. 2:9). She willingly confessed her faith in the living God and proved her faith by her works. Alas, many people hear the Word and tremble but never act upon what they know. Even demons can do that (James 2:19)!

In one of his early sermons (1857), Charles Haddon Spurgeon described Rahab's faith in an alliterated outline, something unusual for him. Her faith was:

saving faith

singular faith—she alone was delivered with her family

stable faith—nothing moved her

self-denying faith—"She dared to risk her life for the sake of
    the spies"

sympathizing faith—she wanted mercy for her family as well

sanctifying faith—she never returned to being a harlot

CHS, 3:97–104

In a later sermon focusing on the scarlet cord from the window
(Josh. 2:17–21), Spurgeon saw Rahab as an example of a true
believer (55:516–28). She had obedient faith and immediately
tied the cord from the window. She believed the promise that the
spies made to her and proved her faith by her works. She made
an open declaration of her faith. Her whole house was dedicated
to the Lord.

In a third sermon, Spurgeon amplified the uniqueness of Rahab's
faith. She was not in a believing nation, her parents had given her
no instructions, and her knowledge of the true God was very slen-
der. What she had to believe was very difficult—that the Jordan
River would open up so the Israelites could cross, and that the
strong city of Jericho would fall. However, Spurgeon believed that
as great as her faith was, it was still flawed because she lied to the
men who asked about her visitors. "But at the same time, please
to recollect that she did not know that it was wrong to lie."

CHS, 18:397–408

Rebekah

[T]he first reference to her domestic life is one of the sweetest in the
annals of womanhood. It is contained in a single sentence, stating
that she supplied to Isaac the place of his deceased mother (Gen.
24:67). The heart of Isaac had been overshadowed by the death of
Sarah; Rebekah crept into the vacant spot and rekindled the ashes
on the scene of the vanished fire. Rebekah's first love for Isaac was

a mother's love. It is a great mistake to imagine that maternal love is
something which can only exist between mother and child. There is
many a woman whose attitude to her husband is instinctively that
of motherhood. Not seldom is the feminine nature the stronger.
Where it is, female love takes the form of protectiveness.

GM-RWB, p. 83

[S]he watches the growth of her two boys and she makes a dreadful
discovery. She finds that her firstborn is utterly unfit for the great
destiny that lies before him . . . she sees that Jacob and not Esau
is the man for his father's priesthood. . . . If she wants Jacob to be
the heir, it is not because her heart yearns for him, it is because her
heart yearns for the God of her clan. . . . Has she not observed how
Jacob clings to the clan of Abraham and how Esau associates with
the children of Heth! Has she not pondered how Jacob worships at
the altar of God while Esau spends time in the hunting-field!

GM-RWB, p. 87

[Genesis 27] I have always recognized this incident as the one
blot of her life. A blot it certainly was—deep, dark, disconcerting.
But it is none the less a blot with pure ink and the very ink with
which she is writing her life. This woman's sin was not, as most
sins are, the fall *from* an habitual path of righteousness; it was a
fall *in* her habitual path of righteousness. David fell by revolt from
God, Solomon fell by forgetting God; but Rebekah fell by fanati-
cism for God. . . . Rebekah's darkest deed came from the sense
that she was obeying the Divine Will. She never dreamed that she
was working for any end but the cause of Providence. She was
wrong, as Saul of Tarsus was wrong.

GM-RWB, p. 91

Rebekah desired nothing for herself, but everything for Jacob: for
him spiritual blessing—at all events, temporal distinction. She did
wrong, not for her own advantage, but for the sake of the one she
loved. . . . Throughout the whole of this revolting scene of deceit
and fraud, we can never forget that Rebekah was a mother.

F. W. Robertson, *Sermons*, 4:127

Beware of that affection which cares for your happiness more than
for your honor.

F. W. Robertson, *Sermons,* 4:131

Faith is living without scheming.

Reuben (Gen. 35:22; 49:4)

That sin deprived him of the primacy—*that one sin.* Was not this
arbitrary? Not so: since it was the index of his character, and was
the unerring evidence of an unstable nature, for sensuality and
instability are one.

Meyer, *Israel,* p. 151

Ruth

Judges is the book of "no king" (Judg. 17:6; 18:1; 19:1; 21:25) when
people did whatever they wanted to do and the nation was in a
mess. We are living today in the book of Judges, for there is no King
in Israel. First Samuel is the book of man's king, when the nation
asked for a king and God gave them Saul. It's obvious that Saul
was never meant to establish a permanent dynasty because he did
not come from the royal tribe of Judah (Gen. 49:8–12). God used
Saul to discipline the nation and make them long for something
better. Second Samuel is the book of God's king—David—and the
book of Ruth tells us where he came from. David is a type of Jesus
Christ, and as we pray "Thy kingdom come," we long for the Lord
Jesus to return and establish his glorious kingdom.

WWW

The book of Ruth takes place during the period of the judges. It
is hard to believe that in such turbulent and decadent days, God
could be working in Israel, but he was—and he is today. Ruth
is the key character in a beautiful love story, reminding us that
Jesus is calling his Bride today in spite of what the wicked society
is doing. But Boaz is not only the bridegroom, he is also the lord

of the harvest, just as Jesus today is reaping a harvest of those who trust him. Whenever we get cynical and critical because of the mess this world is in, we should read the book of Ruth and remind ourselves that God is at work getting a Bride for his Son and reaping a harvest of souls.

WWW

God is named twenty-five times in eighty-five verses. The providential hand of God is seen throughout the entire book. Men may be disobeying the Lord, but God is still at work in the land.

Being a Moabitess, Ruth was not allowed to enter into the nation of Israel (Deut. 23:3), but she put her faith in Jehovah (Ruth 1:16–17; 2:20) and surrendered to the Lord of the Harvest (Ruth 3:8ff).

Every language spoken among men has its own stock of cruel proverbs and satires and lampoons at the expense of their mother-in-law. But Ruth and Naomi go far to redeem that relationship from all that obloquy.

AW-BC, p. 202

The women are so delightful in this delightful little book that there is no room for the men. The men fall into the background of the Book of Ruth, and are clean forgotten.

AW-BC, p. 205

From gleaning in his fields, and from falling at his feet, on till she sat at his table and lay in his bosom—Ruth from first to last had nothing in her heart but pride and respect and love for Boaz. . . . With all that, it is not at all to be wondered at that the Church of Christ, with such a dash of romance and mysticism in her heart, should have seen in Ruth's husband, Boaz, a far-off figure of her own Husband, Jesus Christ.

AW-BC, pp. 206–7

[Ruth 1:16] This was a very brave, outspoken confession of faith. Please to notice that it was made by a woman, a young woman, a poor woman, a widow woman, and a foreigner. Remembering all that, I should think there is no condition of gentleness, or of obscurity, or of sorrow, which should prevent anybody from making an open confession of allegiance to God, when faith in the Lord Jesus Christ has been exercised.

CHS, 46:289

All literature abounds in love stories; but this is the only instance of a great love story about a mother-in-law and a daughter-in-law. Too often that relationship has been the theme of vulgar jest and jibe, but here in the Book of Ruth it is lifted into the heavenly places. . . . But it was more than her mother-in-law and her mother-in-law's people and land, that Ruth chose. She chose Naomi's God. "Thy God shall be my God."

CEM, *Way of a Man,* p. 25

S

Samson

What more could God, or man, or angel of God have done for Samson that was not done? . . . From his birth, and for long before his birth, the gifts of God were simply showered on Samson. He had a father and a mother of the very best.

AW-BC, p. 196

The name "Samson" means "sunny, sunshine," and yet he ended up in darkness.

Samson was chosen by God to *begin* the work of defeating the Philistines (Judg. 13:5). This work was continued by Samuel (1 Sam. 7:13) and completed by David (2 Sam. 8:1; 19:9).

Samson, however, though he had great physical strength, had but little mental force, and even less spiritual power. His whole life is a scene of miracles and follies. He had but little grace, and was easily overcome by temptation. He is enticed and led astray. Often corrected, still he sins again.

CHS, 4:474

You go out, like Samson, against the enemies of God and His Church, but all the time you make your campaign an occasion for your own passions, piques, retaliations, and revenges.

AW-BC, p. 198

And yet he failed, as many another has failed, partly because he persuaded himself that restraint in one direction allowed license

170

in others; partly because he trusted to the outward sign of his consecration to carry him through.

G. H. S. Walpole, *Personality and Power,* p. 146

Samson got out of touch with God *unconsciously through presumption.* King Saul got out of touch with God deliberately through disobedience.

J. Oswald Sanders, *The Cultivation of Christian Character,* p. 42

So accustomed did Samson become to the cooperation of the Spirit, that he grew presumptuous, and trifled with the secret of his strength.

Sanders, *The Cultivation of Christian Character,* p. 44

He played with his enemies as a lion plays with its prey. His full, frolicsome life breaks out in all he does. He is a great, good-natured boy, passionate and excitable, but susceptible and impulsive, and apparently keeping no strong hatred even for the people whom it was the mission of his life to punish.

Phillips Brooks, *The Law of Growth,* p. 255

Dr. James Stalker finds six classes of the tempted, three on the right and three on the left. On the left are those that are being tempted, those that are yielding to temptation, those that are leading others to temptation. On the right are those that are resisting temptation, those that have outgrown some temptations, and those that are helping others to overcome temptation.

A. T. Robertson, *Passing on the Torch,* p. 159

Samson's loss of strength came soon after his greatest exploits. Pride goes before a fall. Victory can demoralize an army as readily as defeat.

A. T. Robertson, *Passing on the Torch,* p. 158

[Judges 16:21] The blinding effects of sin, the binding effects of sin, the grinding effects of sin.

[Judges 13:23–31] They thought they were summoning their *fool,*
these thousands. They did not know they were summoning their
fate.

GHM, *Footsteps of the Flock,* p. 123

For God's watchmen to become the world's showmen is a miserable business.

CHS, 37:87

[Judges 16:28] "Only this once!" That was the remarkable thing in that
final prayer of Samson, "O Lord, remember me and strengthen me,
only this once." That phrase in Samson's prayer suggests the power
of one sincere prayer, one right decision, of one quick obedience to
the Spirit of God, of one turning to God, one act of repentance.

CEM, *Chariots of Fire,* p. 111

It was not an elevated prayer, but is, like all the rest of his actions
at their best, deeply marked with purely personal motives. The
loss of his two eyes is uppermost in his mind, and he wants to be
revenged for them.

Alexander Maclaren, *Expositions of Holy Scripture,* 2:256

[Judges 13:25] What text shall we write on that sequestered grave?
Jeremiah 9:23–24.

GHM, *Footsteps of the Flock,* p. 123

At first thought the life of Samson impresses one as a wasted life.
But Samson never fell altogether away from God. He knew where
the secret of his great strength lay. We take this final prayer of
Samson as a token of his genuine repentance. In his life and in his
death he rendered great service to the people of God. The writer
of the Epistle to the Hebrews puts Samson among the heroes of
the faith (Heb. 11:32).

CEM, *Chariots of Fire,* p. 115

But man's extremity is God's opportunity. And in such words as
were possible to Samson's Old Testament biographer, that sacred
writer tells us that in Samson also, where sin abounded, grace did

much more abound, and that God's strength was made perfect in the day of Samson's weakness.

AW-BC, p. 200

Samuel

He was the last of the judges and the first of the prophets for that new era in Israel's history (Acts 3:24; 13:20; Heb. 11:32).

[1 Samuel 3] It was needful that he should *exchange the traditions for the experimental* [experiential]. His faith must rest, not on the assertions of another's testimony, but on the fact that for himself he had seen, and tasted, and handled the Word of life [1 John 1:1–3]. Not at second-hand, but at first, the Word of the Lord must come to him, and be passed on to all Israel.

Meyer, *Samuel,* p. 29

Samuel was asleep, yet he heard God's voice. But I know some people who are awake, yet have not heard it.

CHS, 54:110

Compare 1 Samuel 2:26 with Luke 2:52.

[1 Samuel 2] Samuel grew up at a time when the spiritual life of the land was at low ebb, and in a home where the father, though a priest, tolerated sin in the lives of his own sons. Eli failed to raise a godly family, yet he succeeded in training Samuel to serve the Lord.

Like his godly mother Hannah, Samuel devoted himself to prayer. See 1 Samuel 7:9, 17; 9:6–12; 12:16–25; 15:11; Psalm 99:6; Jeremiah 15:1.

[1 Samuel 4] They did not realize that God's very present help depended not on the presence of a material symbol, but on moral and spiritual conditions which they should have set themselves to understand and fulfill. [See Jer. 7:12.]

Meyer, *Samuel,* p. 37

[W]hen Saul became king, Samuel was compelled to retire into
obscurity, and become of no reputation. Samuel was emptied
from vessel to vessel till there was no lees [dregs] left in the
wine. The noblest thing, in some respects, in all Samuel's noble
life was the way he took the providence of God in the establishment of the monarchy. The monarchy was a great innovation. It
was a great revolution. And even more than that, it was a severe
condemnation, if not of Samuel's own life, yet of his office and
his order, which are sometimes dearer to a man than life itself.
And, in addition to that, it was the disposition and dismissal of
his two sons from the office and the rank to which he had raised
them. . . . All Samuel's past life had been spent in animating and
purifying, and restoring the republic, but when he saw that a
kingdom was coming in, instead of meeting it with resistance
and obstinacy and lifelong hostility, the great man bowed to the
will of God and the will of Israel, and cast in his lot with the
new dispensation.

AW-BC, p. 225

It takes the very finest natures to pass over from one generation to
another, and to work in the new generation as they worked in the
old. It was splendidly done by Samuel. . . . It is only the old, and
the ripe, and the much-experienced, and the men fullest of past
service, who can do Samuel's service to our generation and the
generation which is coming up after us. . . . But Samuel, deposed
and superceded as he was, was full of new and still more fruitful
ideas for Israel. And what did Samuel do to occupy his talents in his
ripe age, and still to serve God and God's people? Never mortal man
did a better, or a more fruitful thing than Samuel now did. Samuel
planned and set up an institution, so to call it, that has made far
more mark on the world than anything else that survives to us out
of Israel or Greece or Rome. In his ripe and farseeing years, Samuel
devised and founded and presided over a great prophetical school in
his old age. That school of the prophets to which we owe so much
of Samuel himself; to which we owe David, and Gad, and Nathan,
and all their still greater successors; that great school was the creation
and the care of Samuel's leisure from office. How much of the Old
Testament itself we owe to the prophets, and the preachers, and

the psalmists, and the sacred writers, and other trained students of Samuel's great school, we have not yet fully found out.

AW-BC, p. 226

But, crowning all and sanctifying all was Samuel's life of prayer. Samuel was a proverb of prayer. The tradition of Hannah's psalm and prayer was well known to every young prophet in Samuel's school, and her best memories were perpetuated and transmitted in the devotional life and labors of her son. "Moses and Aaron among His priests, and Samuel among them that call on His name" (Ps. 99:6). As much as to say that Samuel stands at the head of all the men of prayer in Israel, just as Moses and Aaron stand at the head of all the prophets and priests in Israel. . . . "As for me," said Samuel, "God forbid that I should sin against the Lord in ceasing to pray for you" (1 Sam. 12:13).

AW-BC, pp. 227–28

Clovis Chappell entitled a sermon on Samuel "The Man Who Refused to Be Fired." See his book *Meet These Men*, pages. 28–38. In another sermon on Samuel, in his book *And the Prophets,* he said: "This wise prophet became peculiarly interested in the youth of his day. There are few surer signs that one has grown old and sour on the inside than his wholesale condemnation of youth. Because of his keen interest in youth, Samuel ceased to speak only the language of the generation into which he was born. He began also to speak the language of another generation. He found young men hungry for God, but too ignorant to know how to find him and how to interpret him to others. For these he established divinity schools. All the theological seminaries that have been built since that far-off day had, in a sense, their beginning here" (p. 40).

On the schools of the prophets, see 1 Samuel 10:3–5; 19:20–24; 2 Kings 2.

On Samuel and the witch of Endor, see Saul.

Sarah (Genesis 12–23; see also Isa. 51:2; Rom. 4:19; 9:9; Gal. 4:22–31; 1 Peter 3:6)

Even though she laughed when she heard the Lord's announcement that she would bear a son (Gen. 18:9–15), and then lied about her laughter, Sarah was a woman of faith (Heb. 11:11) and an example of obedience (Gen. 16:12; 1 Peter 3:6). She was wrong when she gave Hagar to Abraham (Gen. 16) but right when she told Abraham to dismiss Hagar and Ishmael from the camp (Gen. 21:8–21, note v. 12). She symbolizes "the heavenly Jerusalem" and the freedom of its children in the new covenant (Gal. 4:22–31). She helped her husband show hospitality to the Lord and two angels (Gen. 18:6). The first mourning and funeral in Scripture involves the death of Sarah, and she is the only woman in Scripture whose age at death is recorded (127; see Gen. 23:1). On two occasions, Abraham jeopardized the Messianic promise by lying about his wife in order to protect himself (Gen. 12:10–20; 20:1ff). It was a selfish thing to do and Sarah willingly cooperated, but the Lord overruled and delivered them both.

WWW

When Abraham made the great venture of faith, renouncing hearth and home for conscience' sake; when he lived a nomad life among strangers, summering and wintering under canvas, enduring trials and afflictions, she was always by his side, lightening the way he traveled, doubling his joys and dividing his sorrows; ordering the peace and comfort of his house, cheering him to face all hardships with constancy of mind, and sometimes in hours of temptation and danger putting him to shame by her quiet-hearted heroism. . . . Sarah was a princess in name and in nature. She understood her husband's divine vocation, shared his religious aspiration, and never ceased to be his true helpmeet.

Strahan, Hebrew Ideals, p. 111

[L]et us note *what a happy circumstance it is when a godly, gracious man has an equally godly, gracious wife.* . . . It is said of her that she did well, "whose daughters you are as long as you do well" (1 Peter

3:6). She did well *as a wife*. . . . She did well *as a hostess*. . . . She did well *as a mother*. . . . She did well *as a believer*.

Summarized from CHS, 27:677–81

[Genesis 18:9–15] When it was announced to Abraham that he should have a son, Sarah was not present, Eastern etiquette requiring a lady of rank to remain in her private apartment during a visit of male strangers. . . . Through the intervening curtain she listened to the promise, and laughed at it with bitter incredulity. It sounded [more like] irony than truth, and awoke in her the spirit of doubt and denial. But when she heard the Guest rebuke her secret laughter, and expose the dissimulation into which she was then betrayed by fear, and ask in tones which seemed more than human if anything was too hard for God, she was shaken out of her doubt, and restored to the humility of faith. She received the great blessing "because she judged Him faithful who had promised" (Heb. 11:11).

Strahan, *Hebrew Ideals*, pp. 109–10

[Genesis 21:9] Sarah's watchful eye fell upon him [Ishmael] mocking and teasing her son—*Isaac-ing* him—turning the beloved name into a jest. It was not innocent mirth, but unmannerly rudeness and wanton cruelty [Gal. 4:29]. The jealous mother's smoldering wrath was quickly rekindled with the result that she demanded the instant expulsion of the bondwoman and her son.

Strahan, *Hebrew Ideals*, p. 146

[Genesis 23] The presence of death drew from Abraham the pathetic confession, "I am a stranger and a sojourner with you" (23:4). . . . He had never been able to say in Canaan, "I am at home." . . . The thought of life as a pilgrimage sank deep into the Hebrew mind; and even after the Children of Israel had conquered Canaan, and were wanderers no more, but settled owners of the soil, they were still but strangers and pilgrims with God (Ps. 39:12; 1 Chron. 29:15). See also Hebrews 11:8–10, 13–16.

Abraham did not take Sarah's body back to Ur for burial, for he would not return to the place of the old life (Gen. 24:1–9). Nor would he merely abandon the body, or bury it hastily, for Sarah had been his faithful wife and he loved her too much to do that. In spite of his sorrow, Abraham went through the long and tedious bargaining that was so typical of the Eastern peoples. The Hittites respected him, but when Ephron asked far too much money for the property, Abraham still paid it and did not argue. By God's grace, he owned the whole land, but he couldn't explain that to his pagan neighbors; so he paid the full price and maintained his testimony. Sarah's body was the first to be deposited in the cave, but in years to come, others were placed there with her—Abraham, Isaac, Rebekah, Leah, and Jacob. The entire land was Abraham's, but all he owned in it was a tomb. However, should you and I die, we will take nothing with us from this world but will leave behind only a burial place.

WWW

Saul, King of Israel

His character, indeed, is obscure, and we must be cautious while considering it; still, as Scripture is given to us for our instruction, it is surely right to make the most of what we find there, and to form our judgment by such lights as we possess. It would appear, then, that Saul was never under the abiding influence of religion, or, in Scripture language, "the fear of God," however he might be at times moved and softened. Some men are inconsistent in their conduct, as Samson; or as Eli, in a different way; and yet may have lived by faith, though a weak faith. Others have sudden falls, as David had. Others are corrupted by prosperity, as Solomon. But as to Saul, there is no proof that he had any deep-seated religious principle at all; rather, it is to be feared, that his history is a lesson to us, that the "heart of unbelief" may exist in the very sight of God, may rule a man in spite of many natural advantages of character, in the midst of much that is virtuous, amiable, and commendable.

John Henry Newman, *Parochial and Plain Sermons*, 3:35–36

Unbelief and willfulness are the wretched characteristics of Saul's history—an ear deaf to the plainest commands, a heart hardened against the most gracious influences.

Newman, *Parochial and Plain Sermons*, 3:42

Note Saul's fears: he feared the enemy (1 Sam. 13:11; 28:5), his own people (1 Sam. 15:24), Goliath (1 Sam. 17:11), and David (1 Sam. 18:12).

Samuel had grown gray in a service that made all Israel acknowledge and know God from one end of the land to the other; but Saul, all the time, did not know Samuel when he saw him.

WWW

Few have had a fairer chance than Saul. Choice in gifts, goodly in appearance, favored by nature and opportunity, he might have made one of the greatest names in history.

Meyer, *David,* p. 9

He was elected and crowned king over all Israel, but he was as ignorant all the time of the God of Israel as he was of Samuel, the great prophet of the God of Israel. The Spirit of God came upon Saul for outward and earthly acts, but never for an inward change of heart. . . . Saul all along was little better than a heathen at heart.

AW-BC, p. 231

[1 Samuel 9:21] Saul all his days was never so near the kingdom of heaven as when he said to Samuel, "Am I not a Benjamite, of the smallest of the tribes of Israel, and my family the least of all the families of Benjamin?"

AW-BC, p. 232

[1 Samuel 10:9—"God gave him another heart"] Saul has no longer the heart of a husbandman, concerned only with corn and cattle; he has now the heart of a statesman, a general, a prince. Whom God calls to service He will make fit for it.

Matthew Henry

I do not think that he ever did really, in his inmost soul, know the Lord. After Samuel anointed him, he was "turned into another man," but he never became a new man; and the sense of God's presence that he had was not, for a moment, comparable to that presence of God which a true saint enjoys.

CHS, 48:521

Whenever God calls a man to high vocation, it is not merely true to say He will confer upon him what he needs for the fulfillment of that vocation; it is also true that He has chosen the right man for the work. . . . The call of God is always answered by the capacity that lies within a man; it is made to that.

GCM, 9:13

[1 Samuel 11:17–25] If God has called a man to kingship, he has no right to hide away . . . if that man out of any sense of modesty shall hide away and try to escape the responsibility, therein is the first evidence of his weakness. So it was with Saul.

GCM, 9:14

The fundamental wrong of this man was that he failed to submit to the one King. Lack of loyalty to God; that was it. . . . This man in his government of Israel was a warrior and nothing more; he was never a shepherd.

GCM, 9:16–17

[1 Samuel 13] His impatience really amounted to distrust of Jehovah. His presumptuous offering was not really because of concern to propitiate God, but to impress the people.

Baxter, *Mark These Men*, p. 29

[1 Samuel 15] Everything hinges upon absolute obedience. If you cannot obey, you cannot command.

Meyer, *Samuel*, p. 137

[1 Samuel 15:35] Saul's rejection reminds us of other Scriptures. "Ephraim is joined to his idols: leave him alone" [Hosea 4:17]. "He that is filthy, let him be filthy still" [Rev. 22:11]. . . . "Be not Thou silent unto me, O Lord, lest if Thou be silent, I become like unto them that go down into the pit" [Ps. 28:1].

[1 Samuel 18:5–9] It is a dangerous crisis when a proud heart meets with flattering lips.

John Flavel

[1 Samuel 26:21—"I have played the fool"] A man plays the fool if he halts when God calls him to some pathway of service . . . when he neglects his best friends . . . if he marches upon the Divine enterprise when God has not commanded him . . . if he disobeys in even the smallest matter . . . when he attempts to justify the wrong he has done . . . when he allows some hatred to master him, as Saul did in the case of David.

GCM, 9:21–22

It was Saul's folly in consulting the witch of Endor that brought about his death (1 Sam. 28; 1 Chron. 10:13).

[T]he tragedy of King Saul is the tragedy of a man who has been led by the events of his life into a position which he is not qualified to hold. It is the tragedy of a man who is not strong enough and not weak enough to pass through life successfully. He did not have it in him to be master and yet he had it in him not to be satisfied with the second place. . . . It is the tragedy of everyone whose ambition is beyond his endowment.

John Hutton, The Tragedy of Saul, p. 81

"How the mighty have fallen!" lamented David when he received the report of the death of Saul and Jonathan (2 Sam. 1:25, 27), but when Saul began his reign, he was admired for standing taller than any of the people (1 Sam. 10:23). Yet he fell on his sword on the battlefield and took his own life (1 Sam. 31:1–6). "Therefore let him who thinks he stands take heed that he does not fall" (1 Cor. 10:12 NASB).

WWW

Simeon (Luke 2:22–35)

[Luke 2:25] What a biography of a man! How short, and yet how complete! . . . Beloved, that is enough of a biography for any one of us. If when we die, so much as this can be said of us—our name, our business—"waiting for the consolation of Israel," our character—"just and devout," our companionship—"having the

Holy Ghost upon us"—that will be sufficient to hand us down, not to time, but to eternity.

CHS, 11:625

Simeon was led by the Spirit and taught by the Word, and his heart was focused wholly on seeing the Savior. When he saw him, he received him and sang praises to God. Can we find a better example to follow?

WWW

[Luke 2:30] For salvation in that day, as in this day, had as many meanings as there were men's minds. . . . To one man in the temple that day the salvation of God meant salvation from Caesar; while to another man it meant his salvation from himself. To one man it was [salvation from] the tax-gatherer; and to another [from] his own evil heart.

AW-BC, p. 454

Solomon

The shipwreck of Solomon is surely the most terrible tragedy in all the world. For if ever there was a shining type of Christ in the Old Testament church, it was Solomon. If ever any one was once enlightened, and had tasted the heavenly gift, and was made partaker of the Holy Ghost, and had tasted the good word of God, and the powers of the world to come, it was Solomon. If ever any young saint sought first the kingdom of God and His righteousness, and had all these things added unto him, it was Solomon. . . . If ever it was said over any child's birth, "Where sin abounded, grace did much more abound," it was surely over the birth, and the birth-gifts and graces of Solomon.

AW-BC, pp. 278–79

His wisdom as his life went on descended not from above. The wisdom that is from above is first pure, then peaceable.

AW-BC, p. 283

[T]he secret worm . . . was gnawing all the time in the royal staff upon which Solomon leaned.

AW-BC, p. 284

That which lay at the bottom of all Solomon's transgressions was his intimate partnership with foreigners. . . . In the whole Jewish system, no principle was more distinct than this—the separation of God's people from partnership with the world.

F. W. Robertson, *Sermons,* 4:163–64

The world is that collection of men in every age who live only according to the maxims of their time. . . . No marvel if Solomon felt the superior charms of the accomplished Egyptian and the wealthy Tyrian. His Jewish countrymen and countrywomen were but homely in comparison.

F. W. Robertson, *Sermons,* 4:164

The second step of Solomon's wandering was the unrestrained pursuit of pleasure. . . . There was another form of Solomon's worldliness. . . . He had entered deeply into commercial speculations. . . . The truth seems to be, Solomon was getting indifferent about religion.

F. W. Robertson, *Sermons,* 4:166–69

Solomon married many foreign princesses so he could make peace treaties with their fathers and not have to go to war. His father David risked his life to protect the kingdom of Judah, but Solomon preferred to negotiate. In the end, these foreign wives turned his heart away from the Lord and to pagan idols (1 Kings 11; Neh. 13:26). Compromise in one area of life usually leads to deterioration in another area. Some people believe that Solomon was restored to the faith and that the book of Ecclesiastes is his final confession of faith (12:13–14).

WWW

On Monday, April 16, President Harry Truman concluded his first speech to Congress by reading the prayer of Solomon from 1 Kings 3:9, and he concluded with, "I ask only to be a good and faithful servant of my Lord and my people."

David McCullough, *Truman*
(New York: Simon & Schuster, 1992), p. 360

On the grave of Solomon are two epitaphs. The first can easily be read: "His wives turned away his heart after other gods." But if you bend lower and push back the grass and the weeds, you can read there a second inscription, a second epitaph. It is this, and let us never forget it, for we shall all need it: "My mercy shall not depart away from him."

CEM, The Wisest Fool and Other Men of the Bible, p. 19

Solomon may well be described as the wisest fool in the Bible.

CEM, The Wisest Fool, p. 9

Stephen (Acts 6–7; 11:19)

Stephen began as a member of the church in Jerusalem and was chosen to be a deacon and serve tables (Acts 6:5). Each time he finished with that ministry, he went to the synagogue to witness about Jesus (6:8–12). He was treated just as Jesus was treated, for false witnesses lied about what he said and did. But even as his enemies attacked him, his face shone like that of an angel (6:15). They accused him of attacking Moses, but Stephen's face shone just as Moses' face had shone (Exod. 34:29–35; see also 2 Cor. 3:6–18). He bore witness to Christ whose face had also radiated glory (Matt. 17:1–2). He was taken out and stoned to death, rejected by the religious establishment on earth but welcomed into the glories of heaven (7:54–60). This was the third murder in Israel's history: the religious leaders allowed John the Baptist to be killed, they asked for Jesus to be killed, and they themselves killed Stephen. Their sin kept getting worse. Thus, they sinned against God the Father (who sent John the Baptist), God the Son, and God the Holy Spirit (Acts 7:51; see also Matt. 12:31–32). Stephen's address seems to be only a recitation of the history of Israel, but it is actually an *interpretation and application* of that history. He points out that the Jewish people from the time of Jacob had always rejected their deliverers the first time and accepted them the second time. This was true of Joseph (vv. 9–16), Moses (vv. 17–50), and Jesus (vv. 51–53). When Jesus comes again, they shall look upon him, repent of their sins, and receive their promised King (Zech. 12:10–13:1; 14:1ff).

WWW

[Stephen's] whole story is told in two chapters of the New Testament. We watch him live for but one brief day of his life. . . . But he abides long enough to leave his name written indelibly upon our minds and hearts. . . . Dr. Luke's admiration for this gifted young man is very evident. He has one word that he applies to him again and again, and that is the word "full."

Clovis Chappell, More Sermons on Biblical Characters, p. 24

You see that these Apostles were in danger of being sidetracked. They were in danger of giving all their time to work to which they had not been appointed.

Chappell, More Sermons, p. 23

Oh, for a church that the world cannot treat with indifference! Oh, for a band of saints that it is absolutely impossible to ignore! Oh, for a ministry that will divide audiences and communities and cities and continents into those who are either out and out for Christ or out and out against Him. . . . The Church of Jesus Christ can stand any amount of opposition. "The gates of hell shall not prevail against it." But the direst of all dire calamities is for it to become so effete, so powerless, so dead that it is not worth fighting.

Chappell, More Sermons, p. 32

Joseph Parker, at one time the celebrated preacher in London's City Temple, as a young man used to debate on the town green with infidels and atheists. One day an infidel shouted at him, "What did Christ do for Stephen when he was stoned?" Parker replied, "He gave him grace to pray for those who stoned him." Stephen's prayer for those who stoned him was in reality a greater evidence of the power and presence of Christ in his life than any miracle of deliverance would have been.

CEM, The Wisest Fool, p. 139

In the stoning of Stephen there was lost to the Pentecostal Church another Apostle Paul.

AW-BC, p. 585

Stephen—from the Greek *stephanos*—"a victor's crown." See 2 Timothy 4:8 and Revelation 2:10.

T

Thomas

William Barclay called Thomas "the man who became certain by doubting."

Barclay, *The Master's Men*, p. 47

The more of doubt, the stronger faith, I say
If faith overcomes doubt.

Robert Browning, "Bishop Blougram's Apology"

There lives more faith in honest doubt, believe me, than in half the creeds.

Tennyson, "In Memoriam," sec. 96, lines 11–12

If a man will begin with certainties, he shall end in doubts; but if he will be content to begin with doubts, he shall end in certainties.

Francis Bacon, *The Advancement of Learning,* 1.5.8

Doubt is a problem in the mind ("I don't understand") and the heart ("I feel . . ."), while unbelief is a sin of the will ("I will not believe!"). Thomas was willing to go to Judea and die with Christ (John 11:16), so he was not a coward; but the events involving Christ's trial and death were too much for him. Jesus had told his disciples about these events and promised that he would rise from the dead (Matt.16:21; 17:22–23; 20:17–19), but the Word

186

did not sink into the heart of the disciples. Thomas was not afraid to ask a question in the upper room (John 14:5) and apparently accepted the Lord's answer.

WWW

Barclay sees two main lessons in the incidents involving Thomas: (1) Jesus blames no man for wanting to be sure, and (2) certainty is most likely to come to a man in the fellowship of believers.

Barclay, *The Master's Men,* p. 50.

Whatever it was that kept Thomas away, he was terribly punished for his absence. For he thereby lost the first and best sight of his risen Master, and His first and best benediction of peace. He not only lost that benediction, but the joy of the other disciples who had received it filled the cup of Thomas's misery full.

AW-BC, p. 536

Faith is always easy where love and hope are strong. What we live for and hope to see, what we love with our whole heart, what we pray for night and day, what our whole future is anchored upon, that we easily believe, that we are ready to welcome.

AW-BC, p. 538

Let us act upon the faith we have. Let us frequent the places where He is said to manifest Himself. Let us feed our faith on the strong meat of His word. And, since here also acts produce habits, and habits character; let us act faith continually on faith's great objects and operations. And, especially, on our glorified Redeemer. To Thomas He was crucified yesterday. But to us He is risen, and exalted, and is soon to come again.

AW-BC, pp. 538–39

It is a sad day for any congregation when its own membership begin to absent themselves from its services. . . . Believe me, no community ever loses respect for a congregation till that congregation loses respect for itself.

Chappell, *Sermons on Biblical Characters,* p. 10

Why was Thomas missing? He was missing because he had lost hope. He believed that Christ was dead. He believed that the cause for which he had stood was lost and lost forever more.

Chappell, Sermons on Biblical Characters, p. 12

And just see what this man Thomas missed by not being in the little meeting among the ten. First, he missed the privilege of see-ing Jesus. . . . Thomas missed also the gift of peace. Jesus said to those present, "Peace be unto you." . . . The disciples who were there were re-commissioned. . . . "He breathed on them and said, Receive ye the Holy Ghost." And poor Thomas missed also this benediction because he was not with them when Jesus came.

Chappell, Sermons on Biblical Characters, pp. 14–16

[Thomas] would have been a mere name but for John. But John preserves for us three incidents in which Thomas figured promi-nently [John 11:16; 14:5; 20:19–29] with the result that we have as vivid a mental picture of him as of any one of the Twelve. . . . [H]e was a man of *great and unshrinking devotion.* . . . The other disciples were hesitating. The dangers of Judea were frightening them. Even Peter and John were hanging back. But Thomas never wavered in his mind.

J. D. Jones, The Lord of Life and Death, pp. 120, 122–23

He [Thomas] was a man at once cautious and courageous. We speak of Thomas as a skeptic. Yes, but let the word be redeemed from our abuse of it. He was a skeptic. He was a man who was compelled to investigate, to inquire, a man who "would not make his judgment blind," a man who would "face the specters of the mind," and would make no confession of faith, of hope, of con-fidence, unless it were a confession absolutely honest, true to the profoundest convictions of his mind.

GCM, 5:129

Thomas said, "Unless I see what you saw, I will not believe." He did not ask for something other than they had received. He did not ask for some special revelation, denied to the rest. He asked for the same proof, and for that alone.

GCM, 5:130

The chief thing to remember about Thomas is not that he doubted, that he asked for unusual evidence, but that he was convinced, that he believed so thoroughly and enthusiastically as to give expression to the greatest confession in Christian history, "My Lord and my God!"

CEM, *Chariots of Fire,* p. 57

The difference between the rationalist and Thomas is this: the rationalist wants to disbelieve; Thomas wanted to believe. . . . This is the deepest doubt of all, the doubt born of sorrow; that is, the doubt which rises out of the experience of our lives.

CEM, *Chariots of Fire,* p. 59

He was no more skeptical than his colleagues who, when the women reported earlier that day what they saw at the tomb in the rolled-back stone and the undisturbed grave clothes and the angel visitors, said these were "idle tales, and they believed them not."

Roy L. Laurin, *Meet Yourself in the Bible,* p. 204

Notice how Jesus treated Thomas. He was not angry with him. He did not scold him or condemn him. He did not humiliate him before his fellow disciples. He gently and calmly said, "Reach hither thy finger, and behold my hands; and reach hither thy hand, and thrust it into my side: and be not faithless but believing." All Thomas needed was the sight of his Master. He did not need the evidence he had demanded.

Laurin, *Meet Yourself,* p. 207

We owe a debt of gratitude to Thomas, for his inquiry has furnished us with indisputable evidence concerning the resurrection. His experience teaches us a great lesson of faith and as it has been said, "Thomas doubted that we might have no reason to doubt." Let us go away believing.

Laurin, *Meet Yourself,* p. 208

Timothy

When Paul and Barnabas split up because of their disagreement over John Mark, Barnabas took Mark and sailed to Cyprus and Paul took Silas and embarked on his second missionary journey. But he no longer had Mark "as his minister" and he needed somebody to handle the details that can elude even the greatest apostle. Paul found Timothy (Acts 16:1–5) and made him not only his minister but even as his own son in the faith. The Lord is never at a loss to provide laborers if his people pray (Luke 10:2), and Paul had prayed. Timothy was probably converted as a teenager during Paul's first visit to Lystra (Acts 14:6ff) and thus was Paul's beloved son in the faith. It's likely that Timothy saw Paul stoned there and dragged out of the city (Acts 14:19–20; 2 Tim. 3:10–12). Some suggest that Paul may have been taken into the home of Eunice and Lois where they washed his wounds. The name Timothy means "honoring God."

WWW

Timothy was the son of a racially and apparently also a religiously mixed marriage. His mother was "a Jewess that believed" while his father was "a Greek." Such marriages were quite unthinkable by the exclusive standards of Palestine, but in the dispersion they occurred more or less frequently, especially if the husband became a proselyte. If Timothy's father did accept the Jewish God, he must have remained "a proselyte of the gate," refusing to accept circumcision for himself as well as his son. Otherwise Timothy certainly would have been circumcised. The fact that Luke twice called the father "a Greek" (16:1, 3) without any qualifying adjective, as in the case of the mother, strongly implies that he was a pagan.

Hiebert, *Personalities Around Paul,* pp. 99–100

During a gathering of the local assembly, the Spirit of prophecy, speaking through His prophets, pointed out Timothy for special service, thus sanctioning Paul's desire to have Timothy "go forth with him" (Acts 16:3; 1 Tim. 1:18).

Hiebert, *Personalities Around Paul,* p. 102

Timothy was probably between twenty and twenty-two years old at this time. Fifteen years later Paul called him "a youth," a "term applied to men until the age of forty."

Hiebert, *Personalities Around Paul*, p. 103

Timothy was not an apostle; that is made clear in Colossians 1:1. He was never looked upon as a successor to Paul, and he was never portrayed as having the authority of an apostle. Read the letters to Timothy and Titus and notice that such authority remained in the apostolic office and was not conferred on younger ministers. Yet there is authority (cf. 1 Timothy 4:11, 14): it is the authority of the gospel.

William Sanford LaSor, *Great Personalities of the New Testament*, p. 153

Our first responsibility, as was Timothy's, is to guard the faith that is in us (2 Tim. 2:1). . . . The second responsibility that Paul laid upon Timothy was to train up faithful successors (2 Tim. 2:2). . . . The third responsibility was to trust God (2 Tim. 2:19). . . . The fourth responsibility, and by no means the least important, was to stay out of arguments (2 Tim. 2:23–25). . . . All these responsibilities can be summarized in one charge: "Preach the word, be urgent in season and out of season, convince, rebuke, and exhort, be unfailing in patience and in teaching" (2 Tim. 4:2 RSV).

La Sor, *Great Personalities of the New Testament*, p. 155

[2 Timothy 1:1–7] It is not for nothing, you may depend upon it, that Paul gives Lois and Eunice such a first-class certificate for their first-rate methods, and for their signal success in teaching Timothy to read, and so far to understand the Holy Scriptures.

AW-BC, p. 735

"Give attention to reading" (1 Tim. 4:13). This is one of Paul's outstanding exhortations to Timothy. . . . "Reading" in Timothy's day . . . would mean to him very much what is nowadays called expository preaching or "lecturing" as we say in Scotland. [This can also apply to the public reading of the Word of God.]

AW-BC, p. 739

"Rightly dividing the word of truth" (2 Tim. 2:15); this is another of Paul's masterstrokes in these masterly Epistles. And that masterstroke of the Apostle serves to set forth another of the many advantages of the consecutive and comprehensive exposition of Holy Scripture.

AW-BC, p. 740

And "take heed to thyself" (1 Tim. 4:16). . . . Take heed to thy doctrine indeed, but, first and last, take most heed to thyself. Fix thy very best and thy very closest attention on thyself. This is thy main duty as a pastor. . . . For that minister who constantly and increasingly takes heed to himself in his walk and conversation; in preaching better and better every returning Sabbath; in discharging all the endless duties of his pastorate in season and out of season; in holding his peace in controversy; and in a life of secret faith and secret prayer; God Himself will see to it that such an apostolic minister will be imitated and celebrated both as a pattern minister and a pattern man; both before his people and before all his fellow ministers. All that, by the grace of God, may be attained by any minister who sets himself to attain it.

AW-BC, pp. 743–44

"Stir up the gift that is within thee" (2 Tim. 1:16). The word here translated "stir up" really means rekindle. . . . You can see that Paul is not accusing Timothy of having put out his own fire. . . . Paul is not accusing Timothy of misusing his gifts. . . . Nor is Paul urging Timothy to acquire new gifts. He is not urging him to use gifts that he does not possess. He simply presses home upon him the sane and practical duty of using what he actually has. . . . Use the gift that God has committed to you. That is your duty and your whole duty.

Clovis Chappell, *Sermons on New Testament Characters*, pp. 178–79

Why did Timothy need this exhortation from Paul? (1) He needed it because he was in a hard situation. . . . (2) He needed this message because of his youth. (3) Timothy needed this exhortation because he was timid. [See 1 Cor. 16:10.] . . . (4) Timothy needed this exhortation because he was physically weak. What reason does

Paul urge upon Timothy for stirring up his gift? . . . There is great need on account of great opposition. . . . "The days are evil."

Chappell, *New Testament Characters,* pp. 184–86

In spite of weakness and timidity he dared put himself in the hands of his Lord. For his sake he ventured to stir up his gifts. And as he thus obeyed God a new power came into his life, even the power of the Holy Spirit.

Chappell, *New Testament Characters,* pp. 188–89

Of all members of Paul's circle, there was none with whom he formed a closer mutual attachment than Timothy. In six of Paul's letters Timothy's name is associated with his own in the super-scription; in four of these Timothy's name is the only one to be associated with Paul in this way. . . . Timothy's name is associated with his own because Timothy shared his ministry on a permanent footing.

F. F. Bruce, *The Pauline Circle,* pp. 30–31

[Timothy] was one of the large party that accompanied Paul on his last voyage to Judea (Acts 20:4). After Paul's arrest in Jerusalem we lose sight of Timothy. But he reappears with Paul in Rome, if the captivity epistles were composed there (Phil. 1:1; Col. 1:1; Philem. 1). . . . [Paul] gives Timothy a quite remarkable encomium: "I have no one like him, who will be genuinely anxious for your welfare. They all look after their own interests, not those of Jesus Christ. But Timothy's worth you know, how as a son with a father he has served with me in the gospel" (Phil. 2:20–22).

Bruce, *Pauline Circle,* p. 33

Much misunderstanding has often obscured Timothy's position at Ephesus. He was not the pastor of the Ephesian church, for that church was organized under the leadership of its own elders long before Timothy was stationed there (Acts 20:17–35). Nor was Timothy a bishop with ecclesiastical jurisdiction over the churches in that area. Such a position became a later ecclesiastical development. Rather, Timothy was stationed at Ephesus as the personal representative of the Apostle Paul during his absence.

As the apostolic representative, his work did not affect the local organization of the churches. We may liken his work to that of a modern missionary superintendent, commissioned to exercise supervision over a group of national churches.

Hiebert, Personalities Around Paul, p. 111

Certain interpreters, seizing upon some expressions in the letters to Timothy, especially the second, have attributed certain weaknesses of character and even definite failings to Timothy. . . . While no one would claim exceptional strength of character for Timothy, surely such a view misreads the purpose of Paul's fatherly admonitions to his beloved son. Paul's appeals were meant to be preventive rather than corrective measures. They were timely and pertinent in view of the dark future.

Hiebert, Personalities Around Paul, p. 113

Nowhere in the whole range of Biography do we find friendship and companionship employed, on so large a scale, for the highest ends, without the alloy of selfishness or ambition.

John S. Howson, The Companions of St. Paul, p. 289

U

Uzza (1 Chronicles 13)

First, then, we are to consider DAVID'S GREAT FAILURE. . . . [T]here was no failure through lack of multitudes. . . . Neither was there any failure so far as pomp and show were concerned. . . . Neither was there any failure, apparently, as far as the musical accompaniment was concerned. "David and all Israel played before God with all their might. . . ." What was the reason for that failure? [F]irst, there was too little thought as to God's mind upon the matter. David consulted the people, but he would have done better if he had consulted God. . . . One very important omission was that the priests were not in their proper places, [and] they also had a cart, instead of Levites, to carry the sacred ark. . . . Next, I notice that, the first time, there were no sacrifices. . . . All through this incident, we see that there was no taking heed to the commands of God, and to the rules which he had laid down. *The people brought will-worship to God,* instead of that which he had ordained. What do I mean by will-worship? I mean, any kind of worship which is not prescribed in God's own Word. . . . The first commandment may be broken, not only by worshiping a false god, but by worshiping the true God in another way than that which he has ordained. . . . Mark this: if it be not of His appointment, neither will it meet with his acceptance.

CHS, 49:518–21

195

I suppose that Uzza, through the ark having been so long in his father's house, had grown unduly familiar with it, and therefore touched it. Yet it was an express law that even the Levites should not lay a hand upon the ark. They carried it with staves; the priests alone might touch it for necessary purposes. It was for this profanation that "Uzza died before the Lord."

CHS, 49:526

Z

Zacchaeus

The name of the chief was Zacchaeus. That is important to remember, because it means "pure" or "innocent." The man was far
from pure or innocent, as we shall see. But the beauty of the story
is that his meeting with Christ restored him to his better self. The
soil and stain were rubbed off his name, and it stood forth again
in all its clearness and beauty.

CEM, *Great Interviews of Jesus*, p. 53

There was a soft spot still left in Zacchaeus's heart, and that soft
spot was this: Zacchaeus was as eager as any schoolboy in all
Jericho to see Jesus who He was. And like any schoolboy he ran
before and climbed up into a sycamore tree to see Jesus, for He
was to pass that way. And simple things like that, childlike and
schoolboy-like things like that, always touched our Lord's heart.
Of such is the kingdom of heaven. . . . "Curiosity and simplicity,"
says Calvin, "are a sort of preparation for faith."

AW-BC, p. 487

All Zacchaeus's past life, all his real blamefulness, all the people's
just and unjust prejudices, and all the bad odor of Zacchaeus's class,
it did not for one moment turn our Lord away from Zacchaeus's
house.

AW-BC, p. 488

I cannot get out of my mind the deep share that Matthew the publican must have had in the conversion of Zacchaeus. . . . And when Jesus suddenly stopped under the sycamore tree that day and said, Zacchaeus, come down, and when Zacchaeus dropped that moment at our Lord's feet, no one's heart in all the crowd went out to the trembling little tax-gatherer like Matthew's heart.

AW-BC, p. 489

"For the Son of man is come to seek and to save that which was lost" (Luke 19:10). The story ends with this great declaration, and illumines it in a remarkable and perhaps unexpected way. In the story we discover what our Lord meant by seeking and saving. . . . [I]t is the account of one of the last men that Jesus gathered to Himself before His Cross.

GCM, *The Great Physician*, p. 249

We all know that a publican was a tax-gatherer. There were many such, and the rank and file of them were under the direction of chief publicans. Zacchaeus was one of these. The district was under Roman rule. . . . Rome fixed the rate of taxation, and handed the schedule of the same to the man so appointed. . . . The chief publican was required to remit according to that regulation the amount represented by the population. Then Rome closed its eyes. So long as the chief publican rendered the right amount, that is all the imperial government asked. . . . We remember when the publicans went to John the Baptist and said to him: "Master, what must we do? He said unto them, Extort no more than that which is appointed you."

GCM, *The Great Physician*, pp. 250–51

[Luke 19:8] It is of the utmost importance that we understand that in these words Zacchaeus was not telling the Lord what had been the habit of his life, but what he was about to do as the result of that interview. . . . A radical change had taken place in the man. The habit of his life might have been expressed in the word, "I get." He now is saying, "I give." He had entered, mastered by greed. He came out, mastered by grace.

GCM, *The Great Physician*, p. 255

He was looking for the Savior, and the Savior was looking for him, and what a delightful time it was when they met!

Moody, *Words, Work, and Workers,* p. 247

Zedekiah

"The man who cannot say 'No'" is what Charles Spurgeon called this last king of Judah. "Zedekiah was a gentleman of a sort wonderfully common nowadays. A good-natured, easy man; his nobles could get anything they liked from him. . . . He had a great respect for the prophet [Jeremiah]; he liked to visit him, and know what message he had received from God. He did not wish to have it known that he did consult him; but still he liked to steal away in private, and have a talk with the man of God." Spurgeon went on to list the kind of people we have even today who are like Zedekiah. "This softness of character takes different shapes, but it is the same base metal, the same worthless dross, in every case." These people want to know what religion is fashionable, but they never make a profession of faith. They try to stand on both sides of an issue but "are very weak, and apt to yield." He then explained the causes for this kind of person: a general "softness of character" and "a selfish love of ease" that makes them cowards. "The bottom of all is, however, that when a man is thus timid about doing right, and can easily be persuaded to do wrong, there is *a want of the fear of God in him.*"

CHS, 36:674–80

NOTES

Chapter 1

1. Clarence Edward Macartney, *The Wisest Fool, and Other Men of the Bible* (New York: Abingdon, 1949), 5.

2. Clarence Edward Macartney, *The Making of a Minister* (Great Neck, NY: Channel Press, 1961), 131. Macartney died in 1957 and his friend and former pastoral associate Dr. J. Clyde Henry completed his autobiography.

3. For an excellent discussion of this vital theme, see *Spirit, Word, and Story* by Calvin Miller (Grand Rapids: Baker, 1989).

4. Dag Hammarskjöld, *Markings* (New York: Alfred A. Knopf, 1965), 166.

5. Eugene Peterson, *Run with the Horses* (Downers Grove, IL: InterVarsity, 1983), 38.

6. Bill Moyers, *A World of Ideas* (New York: Doubleday, 1989), 504.

Chapter 2

1. Alan Redpath, *The Making of a Man of God* (Westwood, NJ: Revell, 1962), 5. I highly recommend this series of sermons on King David.

2. William R. Inge, *Outspoken Essays, Second Series* (New York: Longmans, Green, n.d.), 185.

3. Moyers, *World of Ideas,* 13.

Chapter 3

1. Phillips Brooks, *The Influence of Jesus* (London: H. R. Alklenson, 1879), 191.

2. Ralph G. Turnbull, ed., *The Treasury of Alexander Whyte* (Westwood, NJ: Revell, 1953), 26.

3. Ibid., 171. This sermon is also found in Whyte's *Bible Characters from the Old and New Testaments* (Grand Rapids: Kregel, 1990), 683.

4. F. W. Robertson, *Sermons by the Rev. Frederick W. Robertson, Fourth Series* (London: Kegan Paul, Trench, Trubner, 1898), 160.

5. L. T. Remlap, ed., *The Gospel Awakening: Sermons and Addresses of D. L. Moody* (Chicago: J. Fairbanks, 1879), 620.

6. Andrew W. Blackwood, *Biographical Preaching for Today* (Nashville: Abingdon, 1954), 130.

Chapter 4

1. For additional suggestions on biographical preaching, see chapter 19 of my book *Preaching and Teaching with Imagination* (Wheaton: Victor, 1994).

2. Charles Haddon Spurgeon, *The Metropolitan Tabernacle Pulpit* (Pasadena, TX: Pilgrim Publications, 1989), 42:565.

3. Ibid., 28:124.

4. Bliss Perry, ed., *The Heart of Emerson's Journals* (Boston: Houghton Mifflin, 1926), 183.

5. George Matheson, *The Representative Men of the Bible: Adam to Job* (London: Hodder & Stoughton, 1902), 4.

6. Plutarch, *The Lives of the Noble Grecians and Romans*, vol. 14 in *The Great Books of the Western World* (Chicago: Encyclopedia Britannica, 1952), 541.

Chapter 5

1. Warren W. Wiersbe, *Your Next Miracle* (Grand Rapids: Baker, 2001).

2. See Charles Haddon Spurgeon, "Confession of Sin—A Sermon with Seven Texts," in *New Park Street Pulpit,* 3:50 (Pasadena, TX: Pilgrim Publications, 1981).

3. See Boreham's five volumes on "Texts That Made Men's Lives," reprinted as *Life Verses* (Grand Rapids: Kregel, 1994).

BIBLIOGRAPHY

Barclay, William. *The Master's Men.* New York: Abingdon, 1959.

Baxter, J. Sidlow. *Mark These Men.* London: Marshall, Morgan & Scott, 1949.

Black, Hugh. *According to My Gospel.* New York: Revell, 1913.

———. *Listening to God.* New York: Revell, 1906.

Blackwood, Andrew W. *Biographical Preaching for Today.* New York: Abingdon, 1954.

Blaiklock, E. M. *Professor Blaiklock's Handbook of Bible People.* London: Scripture Union, 1979.

Booth, William. *Salvation Soldiery.* London: Salvation Army International Headquarters, 1889. Reprint, Oakville, ON: Salvation Army Triumph Press, 1980.

Booth, William and Catherine. *They Said It.* Salvation Army, 1978.

Boreham, Frank W. *Shadows on the Wall.* London: Epworth Press, n.d.

Brooks, Phillips. *The Influence of Jesus.* London: H. R. Allison, 1879.

———. *The Law of Growth.* New York: Macmillan, 1902.

———. *Sermons for the Church Year.* New York: E. P. Dutton, 1895.

Bruce, F. F. *Paul: Apostle of the Heart Set Free.* Grand Rapids: Eerdmans, 1977.

———. *The Pauline Circle.* Grand Rapids: Eerdmans, 1985.

Buechner, Frederick. *Peculiar Treasures: A Biblical Who's Who.* San Francisco: Harper & Row, 1979.

Candlish, Robert S. *Sermons.* Edinburgh: Adam & Charles Black, 1874.

Carey, S. Pearce. *Jesus and Judas.* London: Hodder & Stoughton, 1931.

Chappell, Clovis. *And the Prophets.* Reprint, Grand Rapids: Baker, 1976.

———. *The Cross Before Calvary.* New York: Abingdon, 1960.

———. *Faces About the Cross.* New York: Abingdon, 1941. Reprint, Grand Rapids: Baker, 1971.

———. *Familiar Failures.* Garden City, NY: Doubleday, Doran and Co., 1928.

———. *Meet These Men.* Reprint, Grand Rapids: Baker, 1974.

———. *More Sermons on Biblical Characters.* New York: Richard Smith, 1930.

———. *Sermons on Biblical Characters.* New York: Richard Smith, 1930.

———. *Sermons on New Testament Characters.* New York: Richard Smith, 1930.

———. *Sermons on Old Testament Characters.* New York: Richard Smith, 1930.

———. *Sermons on Simon Peter.* New York: Abingdon, 1959.

Clow, William M. *Idylls of Bethany.* London: Hodder & Stoughton, 1919. Reprint, Joplin, MO: College Press, 1969.

———. *The Secret of the Lord.* London: Hodder & Stoughton, 1911.

Cook, Madison Dale. *Biographical Concordance of the New Testament.* Neptune, NJ: Loizeaux, 1985.

Epp, Theodore H. *Elijah: A Man of Like Nature.* Lincoln, NE: Back to the Bible, 1965.

———. *The God of Abraham, Isaac and Jacob.* Lincoln, NE: Back to the Bible, 1970.

———. *Joseph: "God Planned It For Good."* Lincoln, NE: Back to the Bible, 1971.

———. *Moses, vol. 1: God Prepares and Strengthens His Man.* Lincoln, NE: Back to the Bible, 1975.

———. *Moses, Vol. 2: Excellence in Leadership.* Lincoln, NE: Back to the Bible, 1976.

Gartner, Bertil. *Iscariot.* Philadelphia: Fortress, 1971.

Griffith-Thomas, W. H. *The Apostle Peter.* Grand Rapids: Eerdmans, 1946.

Hammarskjöld, Dag. *Markings.* Trans. Leif Sjoberg and W. H. Auden. New York: Alfred A. Knopf, 1965.

Hastings, James. *The Greater Men and Women of the Bible.* 6 vols. London: Waverly Book Co., 1913–16.

Hauerwas, Stanley, and William H. Willimon. *Resident Aliens.* Nashville: Abingdon, 1989.

Havner, Vance. *Moments of Decision.* Old Tappan, NJ: Revell, 1979.

———. *Why Not Just Be Christians?* Westwood, NJ: Revell, 1964.

Hiebert, D. Edmund. *Personalities Around Paul.* Chicago: Moody, 1973.

Howson, John S. *The Companions of St. Paul.* London: Strahan & Co., 1871.

Huffman, Jasper A. *Judas: The Biography of a Soul.* Marion, IN: Wesley Press, 1958.

Hutton, John A. *The Tragedy of Saul.* London: Hodder & Stoughton, 1926.

Inge, William R. *Outspoken Essays, Second Series.* New York: Longman, Green, n.d.

Jones, J. D. *The Glorious Company of the Apostles.* London: James Clarke, n.d.

————. *The Hope of the Gospel.* London: Hodder & Stoughton, 1911.

————. *The Lord of Life and Death.* London: Hodder & Stoughton, 1919.

Klassen, William. *Judas: Betrayer or Friend of Jesus?* Minneapolis: Fortress, 1996.

Krummacher, F. W. *David King of Israel.* Grand Rapids: Kregel, 1994.

LaSor, William Sanford. *Great Personalities of the New Testament.* Westwood, NJ: Revell, 1961.

————. *Great Personalities of the Old Testament.* Westwood, NJ: Revell, 1959.

Laurin, Roy L. *Meet Yourself in the Bible.* Findlay, OH: Dunham Publications, 1959.

Lee, Robert G. *Glory Today for Conquest Tomorrow.* Grand Rapids: Zondervan, 1941.

Loane, Marcus. *Mary of Bethany.* London: Marshall, Morgan and Scott, 1949.

Macartney, Clarence Edward. *Bible Epitaphs.* Grand Rapids: Baker, 1974.

————. *Chariots of Fire.* Grand Rapids: Kregel, 1994.

————. *Great Interviews of Jesus.* Grand Rapids: Baker, 1974.

————. *He Chose Twelve.* Grand Rapids: Kregel, 1993.

————. *The Making of a Minister.* Great Neck, NY: Channel Press, 1961.

————. *Peter and His Lord.* New York: Abingdon, 1937.

————. *Trials of Great Men of the Bible.* New York: Abingdon, 1946.

————. *The Way of a Man with a Maid.* Grand Rapids: Baker, 1974.

————. *The Wisest Fool: and Other Men of the Bible.* New York: Abingdon-Cokesbury, 1949.

————. *The Woman of Tekoah.* Grand Rapids: Baker, 1977.

Mackintosh, C. H. *Life and Times of Elijah.* Vol. 5 in *Miscellaneous Writings.* New York: Loizeaux, 1945.

Maclaren, Alexander. *Christ in the Heart.* New York: Funk & Wagnalls, 1902.

————. *Expositions of Scripture.* Reprint, Grand Rapids: Baker, 1974.

————. *The Life of David as Revealed in His Psalms.* London: Hodder & Stoughton, 1888.

————. *Week-Day Evening Addresses.* New York: Funk & Wagnalls, 1902.

M'Cheyne, Robert Murray. *Additional Remains.* Edinburgh: William Oliphant, 1846.

Matheson, George. *The Representative Men of the Bible.* 2 vols. London: Hodder & Stoughton, 1902–3.

————. *The Representative Men of the New Testament.* London: Hodder & Stoughton, 1910.

————. *The Representative Women of the Bible.* London: Hodder & Stoughton, 1907.

Meyer, F. B. *David: Shepherd, Psalmist, King.* New York: Revell, 1895.

————. *Israel: A Prince with God.* New York: Revell, n.d.

————. *Joseph: Beloved, Hated, Exalted.* New York: Revell, n.d.

———. *Joshua and the Land of Promise.* London: Morgan & Scott, n.d.

———. *Moses: The Servant of God.* New York: Revell, n.d.

———. *Samuel the Prophet.* London: Morgan & Scott, n.d.

Miller, Calvin. *Spirit, Word, and Story.* Grand Rapids: Baker, 1989.

Moody, D. L. *Moody: His Words, Work, and Workers.* Ed. W. H. Daniels. Chicago: Nelson & Phillips, 1877.

Morgan, G. Campbell. *26 Sermons by G. Campbell Morgan.* 3 vols. Joplin, MO: College Press, 1969.

———. *The Crises of the Christ.* New York: Revell, 1903.

———. *The Great Physician.* New York: Revell, 1937.

———. *Peter and the Church.* Grand Rapids: Baker, 1978.

———. *The Westminster Pulpit.* 10 vols. London: Pickering & Inglis, n.d.

Morrison, George H. *The Afterglow of God.* London: Hodder & Stoughton, 1912.

———. *Flood-tide: Sunday Evenings in a City Pulpit.* London: Hodder & Stoughton, 1904.

———. *The Footsteps of the Flock.* London: Hodder & Stoughton, 1904.

———. *The Gateways of the Stars.* London: Hodder & Stoughton, 1933.

———. *Highways of the Heart.* London: Hodder & Stoughton, 1926.

———. *Morning Sermons.* London: Hodder & Stoughton, 1935.

———. *Return of the Angels.* London: Hodder & Stoughton, 1909.

Moyers, Bill. *A World of Ideas.* New York: Doubleday, 1989.

Nee, Watchman. *A Table in the Wilderness.* Fort Washington, PA: Christian Literature Crusade, 1965.

———. *What Shall This Man Do?* Fort Washington, PA: Christian Literature Crusade, 1961.

Newman, John Henry. *Parochial and Plain Sermons.* Vol. 3. London: Rivingtons, 1885.

Newton, John. *Voice of the Heart.* Chicago: Moody, 1950.

Nicole, Albert. *Judas the Betrayer.* Grand Rapids: Baker, 1957.

Norris, Kathleen. *Amazing Grace.* New York: Riverhead Books, 1998.

Parker, Joseph. *The Ark of God.* London: S. W. Partridge, 1877.

Paxson, Ruth. *Caleb the Overcomer.* Chicago: Moody, n.d.

Peterson, Eugene. *Run with the Horses.* Downers Grove, IL: InterVarsity, 1983.

———. *Traveling Light.* Colorado Springs: Helmers & Howard, 1988.

Pink, Arthur W. *Gleanings in Genesis.* Chicago: Moody, n.d.

———. *The Life of David.* 2 vols. Grand Rapids: Zondervan, 1958.

Redpath, Alan. *The Making of a Man of God.* Westwood, NJ: Revell, 1962.

Remlap, L. T. *The Gospel Awakening: Sermons and Addresses of D. L. Moody.* Chicago: J. Fairbanks & Co., 1879.

Robertson, A. T. *Epochs in the Life of Simon Peter.* Grand Rapids: Baker, 1974.

———. *Passing On the Torch, and Other Sermons.* New York: Revell, 1934.

———. *Some Minor Characters in the New Testament*. Garden City, NY: Doubleday, Doran, 1928.

F. W. Robertson. *Sermons*. 5 vols. London: Kegan Paul, Trench, Trubner, 1898.

Ryle, J. C. *Holiness*. London: James Clarke & Co., 1956.

———. *The True Christian*. Grand Rapids: Baker, 1978.

Sanders, J. Oswald. *The Cultivation of Christian Character*. Chicago: Moody, 1965.

Scherer, Paul. *Facts That Undergird Life*. New York: Harper, 1938.

Smith, Rodney "Gipsy." *As Jesus Passed By, and Other Addresses*. New York: Revell, 1905.

Soltau, T. Stanley. *The God-Pointed Life*. Chicago: Moody, 1966.

Spurgeon, Charles Haddon. *The Metropolitan Tabernacle Pulpit*. 63 vols. Pasadena, TX: Pilgrim Publications, 1989.

Stewart, James S. *The Gates of New Life*. Edinburgh: T & T Clark, 1939.

———. *A Man in Christ*. New York: Harper, n.d.

Strahan, James. *Hebrew Ideals in Genesis*. Grand Rapids: Kregel, 1982.

Thielicke, Helmut. *How the World Began*. London: James Clarke & Co., 1964.

Tournier, Paul. *Guilt and Grace*. New York: Harper & Row, 1962.

Tozer, A. W. *We Travel an Appointed Way*. Camp Hill, PA: Christian Publications, 1988.

Truett, George W. *We Would See Jesus, and Other Sermons*. New York: Revell, 1915.

———. *The Prophet's Mantle*. Nashville: Broadman, 1948.

Turnbull, Ralph G., ed. *A Treasury of W. Graham Scroggie*. Grand Rapids: Baker, 1974.

Whyte, Alexander. *Bible Characters from the Old and New Testaments*. Grand Rapids: Kregel, 1990.

Wiersbe, Warren W. *Classic Sermons on Judas Iscariot*. Grand Rapids: Kregel, 1995.

———. *A Treasury of the World's Great Sermons*. Grand Rapids: Kregel, 1977.

———. *Your Next Miracle*. Grand Rapids: Baker, 2001.

Wilmington, Harold L. *Wilmington's Complete Guide to Bible Knowledge*. 2 vols. Wheaton: Tyndale, 1990.

Young, Dinsdale T. *The Gospel of the Left Hand*. London: Hodder & Stoughton, 1909.

Warren W. Wiersbe is Distinguished Professor of Preaching at Grand Rapids Baptist Seminary and has pastored churches in Indiana, Kentucky, and Illinois (Chicago's historic Moody Church). He is the author of more than 150 books, including *God Isn't in a Hurry*, *The Bumps Are What You Climb On*, and *The Bible Exposition Commentary: New Testament* (2 vols.), *Old Testament* (4 vols.).